To Tami
Love Mum

Everyone Gets to Play

JOHN WIMBER'S TEACHINGS AND
WRITINGS ON LIFE TOGETHER IN CHRIST

John Wimber

D1334242

ampelōn
PUBLISHING
www.ampelonpublishing.com

ISBN: 978-0-9817705-7-4
Printed in the United States of America
Requests for information should be addressed to:
Ampelon Publishing
PO Box 140675
Boise, ID 83714

To order other Ampelon Publishing products, visit us on the web at:
www.ampelonpublishing.com

Cover & inside design: Lisa Dyches — cartwheelstudios.com

Printed on post-consumer recycled paper

Acknowledgements

To Camie Rose and John Richard for allowing your mom to take the time to work on grandpa's works. This is for you, so you will remember part of the foundation you come from. May you both build on what grandpa lived his life for, and know that daddy and I want you to take these things, and go even farther in God's kingdom than we all have. I feel so proud to be your mommy.

— Christy Wimber

CONTENTS

"I'm tired of hearing about the great man of God. I'd rather hear about the great God of man."

- John Wimber

Introduction

In this second compilation of John's writings, there is a theme of the importance of continuing to grow up in Christ and participating in Kingdom work. Whether in family or ministry life, we are called to "press on towards Him," ever becoming more like the one we call King.

John, known for many of his catchy one-liners, would often say, "Everyone gets to play!" In fact this was one of his most famous sayings, referring to the whole body of Christ, finding their place within the body; this was close to his heart. This came from a man who was an accomplished musician, who was a part of a legendary rock band [Righteous Brothers], who was a pastor, evangelist, teacher, worship leader, songwriter, and leader of a Christian Movement [the Vineyard].

Everyone wanted to see John lead worship; to hear John preach; to have John lead the ministry times; but more often than not, John would grab someone that no one else would have picked, and he'd pull them up onto the stage and give them the opportunity to take a risk!

There was a time early on in ministry, where John was leading rather large meetings around the world, where signs and wonders were following him wherever he ministered. At one point, he said to his wife Carol, "I can either get a tent and have a huge revival where I can do this by myself, or I can release it to the people, and equip them to play." He chose the latter. And sure enough one of John's legacies is that he not only loved "doin' the stuff" himself, but loved it even more when everyone around was also participating. It put the ministry back into the hands of the people, rather than the focus being on himself. John not only spoke about everyone getting to play, but he lived it. Time and time again people will tell you how John would take them along, and lovingly encourage, and oftentimes push them into taking risk for God! Personally, I am where I am today because John noticed what was on my life; took me in, and allowed me to "play" all around the world!

May it continue ... and what a privilege to once again participate in passing on the heritage we have been so richly given.

— Christy Wimber

Foreword

I t's all right there in Ephesians 4:1-16.

"One body, one Spirit, one Lord, one faith one baptism, one God and Father of all...who is over all and through all and in all." v. 7 "But to each one of us, grace-lets (gifts) have been given ... as Christ apportioned it ... v. 11 "It was He who gave some to be apostles, some to be evangelists, some to be pastors and teachers to prepare Gods people for works of service (all the gifts or "grace-lets) ... so that the Body of Christ, MAY BE BUILT UP... v. 16 "From Him the Whole body, held together by EVERY supporting ligament, grows and builds itself up in love ...AS EACH PART does its work."

I was raised Catholic and the priests were the only ones who got to play, which meant everyone else was just the "supporting cast". John on the other hand, had no church experience, which meant he had no idea who should or shouldn't get to play a part. But that all changed once he was exposed to the Scriptures. To John, he naturally expected that all of the CHRIST-INS would get to play and therefore no one part of the body would trump another. It made perfect sense to him that we all play our part, which meant that each and every part were vitally important.

This was the reason why John wanted a magazine called *Equipping the Saints*. In the beginning of the Vineyard, the evangelism, healing and power stuff that began started in John first, but he was quickly appalled at the idea it might end there. He was not comfortable with the idea this would not be for all of us. He truly believed with all his heart that "the fun stuff was for all of us" and not just for him. This was actually a fairly rare thought for a leader back in those days as it was usually the "anointed one" who was allowed to be the only healer and it was usually with his small team of prophets and teachers that held the whole thing together. But we knew this was not our call. In fact at one point we knew we could either get a tent or turn around and equip the saints. I was proud of John that he chose the latter. There were several occasions where John made this point in public. I remember one conference in particular where we had several theologians and seminary professors as well as a handful of Pentecostal rock stars who came to 'check everything out,' most likely to find a place for themselves or criticize in one way or another.

And sensing all this, John decided to bring up a group of five small children to help pray. But it wasn't just to pray for anyone; he had them come up to pray for a gentleman who was crippled.

With very little instruction from John he began to walk these young kids through praying for this crippled man.

"Okay, kids ... just tell those legs what Jesus wants them to do"...

And here these five-, six- and seven-year-old children took over. "You legs get straight now!" "You grow right!" "You bad bones be good!"

And of course the legs had to do what the kids were demanding of them as Jesus was involved. With much shaking and jerking, the legs were instantly healed.

John then thanked the kids and invited the experts up to look closely at the miracle that had just taken place. Then John looked and commented to the stunned audience ... "See? Everybody gets to play ... even little children. How complicated is that?"

And that's what we've believed all these years. We tend to complicate what God has simply called us to do as His Church. To John and I, it's never been about the great anointed one, or those who look like they've got it all together; its always been about God using who He desires to use, (usually, the willing) with the importance of keeping the focus on and about Jesus. This was one of John's wonderful traits where he had the ability to not be threatened or self-focused where he couldn't see and therefore value the bigger picture where others got the chance in some way to play.

Carol Wimber

Prologue

J ohn Wimber brought a team to Chorleywood, Herts, England in 1981. We had never even met or heard him before. We knew not what to expect. It was an unforgettable weekend of amazing blessing. Most previous visiting speakers had come with their ministries and then taken them home with them. John came with his ministry and left it with us–he came not only to teach us of the "now and not yet" of the Kingdom of God, but he showed us how healings and miracles were signs of its coming–signs that could be expected to follow such teaching (Hebrews 2:4). He taught about evangelizing, about the gifts of the Spirit–prophecy and tongues, etc–about loving the whole church, about going out to the poor and needy with ministries of mercy. He taught about church planting and church leadership. Mary and I loved him and felt very honoured to be made so welcome year after year, for well over a decade, in their home at Yorba Linda.

John's background as a successful Californian pop-musician, a Quaker evangelist and minister, a Fuller seminary lecturer and international church counselor was unique. His preaching style was laid-back and humourous, his images were captivating and original, his personality folksy, engagingly warm and humble. His substance was biblical, timely and culturally relevant, his message was Christ-centred and glorifying to God, his prayer was "Come Holy Spirit!" He was a joyful risk-taker for the Lord. What an inspiring model and faith builder for any Christian to want to follow! He left our church with a real tingle factor!

He sowed our people with seed-thoughts that we watched grow and flourish. New testimonies, new visions, new resources and new energies followed. Our Faith Sharing teams took the challenges on board and were wonderfully used by God as they went out to churches across the country and the world. At home we began encouraging leaders from other churches in every way we could, and in time, started week-long residential New Wine conferences (across the UK and abroad) designed for church leaders and church families. These grew by the thousands year after year. Out of them were spawned the Soul Survivor conferences for youth and their leaders. These also began to attract their thousands annually from many denominations. A support network has grown up across the country. New song-leaders emerged whose songs have gone round the world. Clergy retreats and central day rallies for women have been convened. All this without even mentioning the encouraging growth of the Vineyard Christian Fellowships in the UK under their own organization–To God be the Glory!

Bishop David Pytches
The Anglican Communion

One

LAYING ALL DOWN
FOR JESUS

"THE GREATER THE SACRIFICE, THE GREATER THE POWER

THAT IS RELEASED."

I first met the principle of Christian sacrifice at Gunner Payne's Bible study, before I became a Christian. I can still remember the night when I first heard the parable of the Pearl. My wife, Carol, and Gunner were talking on and on about some issue, and I was sitting there, bored, not really paying attention. Then Gunner read the passage about the Pearl in the Gospel of Matthew and explained how it referred to our need to be willing to sacrifice everything in our lives for the kingdom: "the kingdom of heaven is like a merchant looking for fine pearls. When he found one of great value, he went away and sold everything he had and bought it" (Matthew 13:45-46).

That got my attention.

"Hold on a second!" I interrupted. "Are you saying that to become a Christian somebody might have to give up everything he has?" "Well, what do you think the text means?" Gunner replied. "I'm not sure," I said. "It sounds like it might mean that. But...." It took me a moment to collect my thoughts. "Well, I know a guy who is a musician. He doesn't know how to do anything but play music. I mean, this guy can't even tie his own shoelaces. Are you saying he might have to give up his career in order to become a Christian? How else could he make a living?"

"Your friend will have to work that one out for himself," Gunner said, knowing of course that we were really talking about me. "But in my opinion, he has to be ready to give up his career because it's a possibility."

After I had this encounter with the Lord about the Pearl and realized I didn't care much about what God wanted from me, sure enough over the next few weeks God began to help me liquidate my assets.

I prayed, "Okay, Lord, you can have my career," and it was as though two giant hands came out of heaven and opened my fingers, and a voice said, "Thank you."

I said goodbye to my music friends and decided to get a regular job. Suddenly I was plunged into the real world, where alarm clocks go off, where people get up and go to work in broad daylight. I had never done this. In a matter of weeks I was working in a factory, clocking in and learning how to relate to normal people. One day I was assigned to clean some oil drums behind the factory. It was hot, filthy, smelly work. It was the most menial task they had, and the reason they had me doing it was that it was about the only thing I could do. I was down inside one of the oil drums when I heard a car drive up.

A familiar voice said, "Where's John Wimber's office?" Reluctantly I came out. There stood one of my old partners from the music business. In his hand was a contract I had signed, and it was worth a lot of money. In order for him to fulfill it, I had to relinquish my part of it.

He just stood there staring at me. I was a mess. I had grease all over me—my hands, my clothes, my face and my hair. Finally he said, "What are you doing here?" I looked at him, and then looked at myself; then I looked at him again, then at myself. I could see myself as I must have looked through his eyes. Right at that moment, I didn't particularly feel as if I had the Pearl. I could not think of a single thing to say. After a long silence I answered him lamely, "God did this to me." His eyes narrowed with a look of resolve, as if to say, "He's never going to do that to me." I felt ashamed.

Obviously what I was doing with my life seemed to be utter foolishness to him. At that moment I could not think of a single persuasive explanation for why God—this God of love, this God that is so great in the Bible, this God that is so nice to so many people—was apparently being so mean to me.

> As I watched my friend drive away, I realized that sometimes there is no way to explain obedience and sacrifice to God to those who do not see the Pearl.

Why had He chosen to treat me this way? As I watched my friend drive away, I realized that sometimes there is no way to explain obedience and sacrifice to God to those who do not see the Pearl. My friend could not see any value at all in the humiliation of my flesh, in God taking me down from a lofty, worldly position and teaching me simple obedience.

Since that day I have found that all through our lives, in our service to God and His people, we will be put in situations where others look at us with disdain because our obedience and sacrifice to God doesn't make any sense to them. But for those who have found the Pearl, it all makes perfect sense. We know that it is worth everything to follow Him, to walk with Him, to serve Him, to lose our lives for Him. It is worth selling everything we own to gain Christ, and be found in Him.

THE FRUIT OF OBEDIENCE

John 14:21 says, "Whosoever has my commands and obeys them, he is the one who loves me. He who loves me will be loved by my Father, and I too will love him and show myself to him."

Obedience deepens our intimacy with Jesus. If we want to know the Father, we must not only love Him, but also obey Him. Scripture is clear that it is important to know the Father through His Word, and if we want to be a part of what the Father is doing and to be able to see where He is moving, then it is clear that we must obey His commands. It's important to not only be biblically literate, but we must also be biblically obedient!

Obedience to Christ shows that we know that He is God, and we are not. It shows we understand that God knows the best for us in all things. When it comes to His direction in our lives, for example, what we need to be careful of is not what could possibly hurt us, or what He has in store for us to accomplish, but rather that it's a process of learning to trust and obey what He shows us. True happiness comes from letting God not only be our Savior but also our Lord.

Obedience also releases the blessings of the kingdom. In Mark 10:28-31, Peter says, "We have left everything to follow you!" And Jesus responds by saying, "I tell you the truth, no one who has left home or brothers and sisters or mother or father or children or fields for me and the gospel will fail to receive a hundred times as much in this present age, and in the age to come."

OBEDIENCE AND TRUST

What is the difference between being totally committed and just having your "toe in the water," so to speak? Trust and obedience. Trust and obedience must go hand-in-hand. That means in difficult, awkward and hard-to-understand circumstances, we choose to trust. Proverbs 3:5-6 says, "Trust in the Lord with all you heart and lean not on your own understanding; in all your ways acknowledge him, and he will make your paths straight."

It's one of the most important texts in the Bible for me. It's something I've gone back to a thousand times. In fact, trust is also an obedience issue. We are commanded to trust the Lord. Therefore, total commitment to Jesus means trusting even when we don't know the why's or how's of what's happening all around us daily.

TO LIVE IS CHRIST

This is the ultimate goal: to be with Jesus forever whether in life or in death.

Philippians 1:19 says, "Yes, I will continue to rejoice for I know that through your prayers and the help given by the Spirit of Jesus Christ, what has happened to me will turn out for my deliverance. I eagerly expect and hope that I will in no way be ashamed but will have sufficient courage so that now, as always, Christ will be exalted in my body, whether by life or by death."

The Apostle Paul had faced death many times. He wasn't just spouting out theory; he was revealing the driving principle of his life.

The Apostle Paul had faced death many times. He wasn't just spouting out theory; he was revealing the driving principle of his life. In Philippians 1:21-26, Paul writes, "For me to live is Christ and to die is gain. If I am to go on living in the body this will mean fruitful labor for me. Yet what shall I choose? I do not know. I am torn between the two. I desire to depart and be with Christ, which is better by far, but it's more necessary for you that I remain in the body. Convinced of this I know that I will remain and I will continue with all of you for your progress and joy in the faith so that through my being with you again, your joy in Christ Jesus will overflow on account of me."

What a philosophy of life! What a profound impact that must have had on the Philippians as they read it! He was not careless or foolish. He wasn't stupid! Paul recognized the enormity of the things he was saying; he was talking out of the context of having those beliefs tested again and again.

How many times had Paul been beaten, nearly drowned, starved and had his life threatened by people who could fulfill those threats? Yet he said, "For me to live is Christ and to die is gain," understanding that when we enter into heaven it is then we will be free from the presence of sin and will be with Jesus forever. This is the ultimate goal: to be with Jesus forever.

OFFER SELF, NOT JUST SERVICE

Some Christians make the mistake of what I call outward obedience. They become focused on their acts of service as evidence of being obedient Christians. This kind of life does not provoke the level of disapproval from some other Christians that a life of service founded on intimate love or passion will.

Think about Mary and Martha in Luke 10:38-42. Martha worked her tail off getting a meal prepared for Jesus and was criticized by Mary. However, Martha complained to Jesus about Mary's behavior. Martha was irritated that Mary put greater emphasis on loving and listening to her Lord than Martha did. When I think about this story, I imagine Martha complaining to Jesus fully expecting that Jesus would affirm her position. However, when Jesus said that Mary had chosen the better part, I am sure Martha saw her self-righteous attitude for the first time.

Of course, God has called us to give our lives to others, and we are to do it passionately, beginning with believers. We are also meant to reach out to and serve those God is drawing to Himself. Our time, money and energy ought to go into these efforts. However, there is danger inherent in service, and it is subtle. Sometimes we Christians substitute service for the offering of ourselves. In other words, obedience to the Lord is not only measured by how much we do for our Savior, but by how we love and obey Him even when nobody's looking.

Many believe they are walking out the Christian life when in fact their lives are miserable because they are living in a way that's inconsistent with the call of God and the revelation of Scripture.

We must obey a higher call if indeed we have heard and discerned it. Many believe they are walking out the Christian life when in fact their lives are miserable because they are living in a way that's inconsistent with the call of God and the revelation of Scripture. No one has ever stopped and told them, "There's more to this than just bowing your knee and praying the prayer."

SACRIFICE AND POWER

When you think of "sacrifice," do you think this has got to be something negative?

Sacrifice should not be thought of primarily in negative terms. The greatest of all Christian virtues is love (1 Corinthians 13:13), and the purpose of the greatest sacrifice ever made was to release the love of God on all men and women. Sacrifice is not an end in itself; we take up our crosses to follow Christ more fully. I might have given up a promising career as a musician, but I gained the infinite joy of knowing God and eternal life. I thought it was a pretty good deal back in 1963, and I still think so today.

Sacrifice also releases power. The greater the sacrifice, the greater the power that is released. The greatest of all sacrifices, the sacrifice of Jesus, has released the greatest power of all. At the very moment of His death, even before the resurrection, the natural realm could not contain the power released from the throne of heaven. The power of the cross invaded every realm of this world. It shook the foundations of the earth. It assaulted the religious realm, ripping open the temple veil from top to bottom, from heaven to earth. It even took on the greatest enemy of all, death, releasing dead and rotting bodies from their tombs (Matthew 27:51-52). This power is available to us as we pick up our crosses daily (Matthew 16:24-25).

Christian martyrdom illustrates the relationship between sacrifice and power. The death of Stephen, for instance, precipitat-

> **The greater the sacrifice, the greater the power that is released.**

ed a release of heavenly power that led to revival and the conversion of Paul (Acts 7:57-8:3). Christian martyrdom is not confined to ancient church history. On an average there are over 300,000 Christians martyred each year in the twentieth century.

Martyrdom is far from being the only form of sacrifice that releases God's love and power. Excepting martyrdom, the highest form of sacrifice is celibacy, forgoing the joy and security of marriage and family to be a special companion to Jesus. Jesus spoke of those who made themselves eunuchs for the kingdom of God (Matthew 19:12), and Isaiah said that faithful eunuchs would have in God's temple "a memorial and a name better than [that of] sons and daughters" (Isaiah 56:5). A person who is gifted and called to a life of celibacy is free from the normal distractions of marriage and family; he or she can be totally devoted to the things of the Lord (1 Corinthians 7:32-35).

For those of us who are not called to celibacy, God has provided other means of sacrifice. At the top of the list stands prayer and fasting. The power released by prayer is truly amazing. Prayer is the instrument God will use to open or shut the heavens (James 5:16-18). When prayer is combined with fasting, whole armies can be defeated (1 Samuel 7:6-13; 2 Chronicles 20:1-30). Even the judgment of God on evil people can be turned back through prayer and fasting (1 Kings 21:27-29; Jonah 3:5-10), and through it the power of the devil and his own demons is overcome (Matthew 4:1-11).

Finally, giving money and material possessions to the poor and to God's work is a powerful form of sacrifice. Giving that is motivated by love for God and His purposes releases great power and secures blessing (Philippians 4:18-19). The centurion Cornelius "gave generously to those in need and prayed to God regularly," which caught the Lord's attention (Acts 10:2). An angel appeared to Cornelius in a vision, commended him for his generosity and prayer life and directed him to contact Peter, which opened the gospel to the Gentiles.

A WORTHY SACRIFICE

The prospects for the future King of Israel seemed bleak. David had fled from King Saul and was holed up in a cave with a motley crew of mercenaries and discontents. The despised Philistines were in control of Bethlehem, his hometown. In a moment of nostalgia mixed with thirst, David said "Oh, that someone would get me a drink of water from the well near the gate of Bethlehem!" Without being told to do so, three of David's "mighty men" embarked on a hazardous mission without any military objective. They broke through the Philistine lines, drew water from the well of Bethlehem and carried it back to David. An audacious act! But David refused to drink it.

Why? For David, only God was worthy of such a sacrifice, so he poured the water out before the Lord. "Far be it from me, O Lord, to do this!" he said. "Is it not the blood of men who went at the risk of their lives?"

The Bible has much to say about sacrificial living as it relates to you and me. Sacrifice is at the very core of God's nature: out of love for us the Father sacrificed His only Son; out of obedience to His Father, the Son denied Himself and gave His life up for us; the Holy Spirit deflects attention from Himself and glorifies the Father and the Son in us.

Jesus told the disciples, "If anyone would come after me, he must deny himself and take up his cross and follow me" (Matthew 16:24). He then said, "Whoever loses his life for me will find it" (16:25). Paul, echoing Christ's words, says, "I urge you therefore brothers, in view of God's mercy, to offer your bodies as living sacrifices, holy and pleasing to God" (Romans 12:1). Our whole lives are meant to be a sacrifice to the Lord.

Two

Learning to Love

"WE'RE ALL JUST ONE VEGETABLE
IN GOD'S STEW."

One of the greatest legacies John left us is the importance of loving the whole Church. Towards the end of John's life, he spoke of the importance of being a good churchman; however, one of the greatest traits John carried was instead of being "threatened" by the whole Church, he chose to love.

John wrote the following article, addressing leaders in the Vineyard, concerning the Vineyard Movement and the course between chaos and traditional denominationalism that I believe is an important aspect of our foundation. Here is an excerpt from that article that also contains John's strong belief in the unity in the Body of Christ.

— **Christy Wimber**

———◆———

In 1984, the number of Vineyard churches was growing rapidly. We made the decision to formalize the structure that had evolved. Until then we really worked under Vineyard Ministries International, but VMI was a renewal organization, so we then formed AVC [Association of Vineyard Churches]. Historically, we probably became a denomination when we incorporated AVC, appointed Regional overseers, called a board of directors and began ordaining ministers.

And because 99 percent of the churches have the word "Vineyard" in their name, and because of a unified identity, yes, we've become a denomination. Admittedly, I have mixed feelings about that.

Years ago I talked about explorers and homesteaders in the Vineyard. I said at that time that explorers are radicals and usually spin out because they can't stand the containment of an organization. Explorers seek adventure. Homesteaders, on the other hand, build community, leaving a heritage for future generations. Homesteaders use, need and create structure, and by the way, they also create wealth! A few explorers who started out with the movement have not stayed with it because they saw the encroachment of more structure, and they resisted control.

As an organism, the Vineyard needs organization. Compare two life forms: an amoeba and a human body. Which can accomplish more?

Certainly the more highly structured human body (if it is alive). The key is life and relationship with God, not organization or lack thereof.

To father children and not take responsibility for raising them is considered uncivilized. To make new converts and not set them into a church is unthinkable. Likewise, to plant new churches and not band them together and mature them is irresponsible.

But I also believe that it's important to introduce structure carefully always being aware that the organization is subservient to the organism.

No one wants to join something he has to be subservient to. We want to join something that will help us realize our potential. In the past when pastors have asked us, "What are we building here? What am I signing up for?" I would talk about the Vineyard as something that would help leaders do more together than they could do independently.

The organization is subservient to the organism.

Calling the Vineyard a denomination sends up red flags for some of our brethren. The word "denomination" denotes sectarianism, separation and factionalism, and a distorted view of the unity of the Body of Christ. Therefore, it's valuable to remind ourselves that the unity of the Church is an important theme in the Bible, beginning in the Old Testament.

In the Old Testament, Genesis records God creating by His will the world as an ordered unity, in which all creatures satisfy the Creator's purposes. "God saw all that He had made, and it was very good" [Genesis 1:31]. When Adam and Eve sinned and alienated themselves from God and from one another, God acted to bring about mankind's reconciliation. God ordained a covenant with the Hebrew people and united the various tribes into one religious nation, Israel, bridging the alienation between God and the humans and reconciling His people. Ancient Judaism, therefore, stood on the truth of the one people of God. Their faith in the oneness of God [Yahweh] expressed itself in their unity. Psalm 133:1 states, "How good and pleasant it is when brothers live together in unity!"

Their mission was to preserve the faithfulness and unity of all God's people and to prepare them for the fulfillment of the kingdom of God.

In the New Testament, the concept of unity is pivotal to the gospel of Jesus Christ and the teachings of His Apostles. All who confess Jesus as Lord and Savior come together in a new community: the Church. All New Testament writers presume that to be "in Christ" is to belong to one fellowship [Greek: *koinonia*]. Jesus mandated this unity when at the Last Supper He interceded for His disciples, and all those who believe in Him "that all of them may be one, Father, just as you are in me and I am in you. May they also be in us so that the world may believe that you have sent me" [John 17:21]. This unity manifested itself in the miracle of Pentecost [Acts 2] and the historic Council of Jerusalem [Acts 15] that worked out conflicts between Jewish and Gentile Christians.

The early Church, however, was not entirely free from many tensions and conflicts that threatened unity. For example, tensions arose between Jewish Christian churches and Gentile Christian churches, and between Paul and the Judaizers.

Even with diversity and conflicts, historian Paul A. Chow notes, "the early Christians remained of 'one accord,' visibly sharing the one Eucharist, accepting the ministries of the whole church, reaching out beyond their local situation in faith and witness with a sense of the universal community that held all Christians together."

As Paul taught the Ephesians, God's supreme purpose is "to unite all things in Him [Christ], things in heaven and things on earth" [Ephesians 1:10].

Through centuries of sectarianism and fracturing, most Christians today allow differences to divide rather than appreciating and celebrating our distinctions and diversity. Our relations as an extended family are typically clouded by distrust and disrespect.

I want to relate to the whole Body of Christ. Biblical unity to me flows from learning to love what Jesus loves—learning to love the whole Body of Christ. When I cross paths with a brother or sister in a group or denomination different from my own, I want to fellowship based on our shared allegiance to the Lord Jesus Christ. I want to see the Vineyard work through this question: "How can brethren major on the things we agree on, ignore the things we disagree on, and move forward together?" In my opinion, that applies inside and outside the Vineyard.

Are denominations in conflict with unity? Well, first I believe it's important that we look at the definition of what a denomination means. According to Webster, it is a class or society of individuals called by the same name, especially a religious group or a community of believers called by the same name.

In an ideal world, there would be no denominations. But we can't turn the clock back on five hundred years of history. In contrast to a denomination, denominationalism is the emphasizing of denominational differences to the point of being narrowly exclusive. A synonym is sectarianism. Denominationalism promotes one denomination over the rest of the Church and asserts that "our group" is better than any other group.

> **I can totally make my peace with the reality of different denominations, but I totally reject the idea of denominationalism.**

I can totally make my peace with the reality of different denominations, but I totally reject the idea of denominationalism.

Recently I met with a group of Baptist pastors from Scandinavia. I'm not a Baptist, but I love them because they're my brothers. We have relationship, fraternity and fellowship. I am a Christian, and so are they, but I don't have to express it in the mode they do. That's not separation. Separation is when I declare your "brand" of Christianity is inferior to mine because of what you belong to and what you avow or are committed too.

A denomination devoted to sectarianism can have correct theology and have wrong attitudes towards the rest of the Body of Christ, which is an emphasis on "do it our way or take the highway."

We must remember that we can become so enamored of who we are and what we do...and that's a mistake, in my opinion. It's reminiscent of the Tower of Babel in Genesis 11:4, "so that we may make a name for ourselves," which when emphasized produces divisiveness.

This divisiveness results from leaders cultivating sinful attitudes towards other members of the Body of Christ. However, you don't have to be in a denomination to take on this attitude. I have asserted that many groups, individual churches and leaders who do not regard themselves as denominations are quite divisive. What I am saying is that division is not so much a structural problem as an attitudinal one. It can affect an individual Christian as much as a group.

Leaders need to take risks and continue to grow in the same way we took risks and continued to grow. If they don't, God will hopefully raise up some other renewal movement, and they will be seen as irresponsible radicals in much the same way some parts of the institutional church regard the Vineyard today.

Remember, Church history reveals a cycle in which the homesteaders of one renewal movement persecute the pioneers of the most recent move.

> Remember, Church history reveals a cycle in which the homesteaders of one renewal movement persecute the pioneers of the most recent move.

The Methodist movement began a sectarian protest against the worldliness of the Church in England: its success stimulated it to become a church which in turn spawned various sectarian protests, including charismatic communities. The Catholic Charismatic renewal was persecuted by the Pentecostals because the Pentecostals couldn't believe the Catholics were Christians.

If we're not diligently humbling ourselves before the Lord, the Vineyard will do the same thing to someone else eventually.

This sinful attitude is often the result of fear. This is because new and different group leaders frighten us, so we attack them, thereby sowing discord, perpetuating the practice of judging people and practices without proper examination. In this situation, slanderous reports confirming our prejudices are often gladly accepted and passed off as fact to others. May the Vineyard never be accused of contributing to that ugliness.

The antidote for this sectarian spirit is exalting the name of the Jesus. Even in the First Century church, the apostle Paul had to plead the case for unity. In Philippians 2, he writes:

"If you have any encouragement from being united with Christ, if any

comfort from his love, if any fellowship with his Spirit, if any tenderness and compassion, then make my joy complete by being like-minded, having the same love, being one in spirit and purpose. Do nothing out of selfish ambition or vain conceit, but in humility consider others better than yourselves. Each of you should look not only to your own interests, but also to the interests of others" [vv. 1-4].

This applies both locally and globally. The essence of learning to love the rest of the Church is learning how to love one another. We can't do one without the other. I don't want to make a name for ourselves. The Vineyard is not the issue. We need organization to exist—God called us, and I'm not ashamed of us—but the issue is the Body of Christ.

We must lift up no other name but the hallowed name of Jesus. God is passionate for the glory of His own name and will not yield to any man or group. If we don't keep buttressing and encouraging relationship with God first and each other second, we will indeed evolve into a sectarian organization.

DIVERSITY IN UNITY

One illustration of diversity within unity is the twelve tribes of Israel. Each tribe had a different name and a different identity. Jacobs's prophetic blessings in Genesis chapter 49 describe different destinies for each tribe descending from his son. Each tribe was unique.

However, in unity the twelve tribes formed one nation without losing their identity. As long as the tribes were united in purpose (i.e. serving Yahweh), things went well. But in time, as the spiritual vitality of the nation waned, individual tribes sought advantages for themselves rather than the welfare of the nation. Eventually the northern tribes [Israel] were enemies of the southern tribes [Judah].

Without trying to justify denominations from Scripture, I see denominations are to strike a balance between the whole Body and their individual distinctions. Our differences may cause us pain, but they needn't polarize and alienate us. I may not agree with everything about Catholic doctrine, but there's a lot about individual Catholics I love. Our understanding of Scripture may prevent us from endorsing certain doctrines without causing us to despise other traditions in the Body of Christ.

All separation of the Body of Christ is unbiblical, whether denominational or nondenominational. We need to be careful not to think more highly of the Vineyard than we ought, "...but rather think of yourself with sober judgment, in accordance with the measure of faith God has give you" [Romans 12:3]. The Vineyard is simply an experiment in a long line of experiments to live out Christianity within the larger Church.

We need to cultivate an attitude that rejoices in the unique contributions various denominations, movements and traditions have made and currently make to the cause of Christ.

THE DISEASE OF PHARISAISM

As a committed Christian and minister for many years, there is nothing I want more than to be like Jesus! Each time I read the New Testament and see Jesus' compassion, wisdom and power as He interacts with people, I renew my desire once again to be like Him.

Yet along with my prayers and pursuit of being conformed to Jesus' image have come a most disturbing realization: on many occasions there is little resemblance to Jesus in the way I treat people. Recently a woman who had been previously divorced phoned me and asked me to marry her and her fiancee. I responded with a thoroughly correct Biblical proof text and a swift "no." She and her fiancee did get married, and he subsequently became a Christian. I had felt I was safe and correct in my answer, but God corrected me. He impressed me with this thought: "You were wrong John. I had a plan for this man's salvation, and you were supposed to be a part of it."

> Yet along with my prayers and pursuit of being conformed to Jesus' image have come a most disturbing realization: on many occasions there is little resemblance to Jesus in the way I treat people.

I saw that although my answer had been biblical, my attitude of quickly dismissing this woman's request was wrong. I had not stopped to pray, to seek God's direction, or to give sensitive consideration to this woman. I simply made a quick and glib judgment based on a superficial application of Scripture. Though God's plan for the man's life was fulfilled anyway, I had missed the blessing of being a part of it, and worst of all, I saw how unlike Jesus I had behaved.

A new Pharisaism abounds in the Body of Christ today. A heartless "show-it-to-me-in-the-Word" philosophy prevails. Armed with our systematic theology notes and a superficial perception of Scripture, we have attacked all manner of the evils of our day. Yet in many of our exchanges with needy people, we have further injured them, attacking the sinner rather than the sin. If we want to wield the sword of the Spirit skillfully, we must first let it work on us [Hebrews 4:12].

Let me illustrate: John 7:53-8:11 is the account of Jesus and the woman taken into adultery. Scholars have debated whether this passage belongs here or in another place in the New Testament. Here we have a confrontation between the Pharisees, noted for their devotion to the Law, and Jesus who said, "...I have not come to abolish the Law and the prophets, but to fulfill them [Matthew 5:17].

The woman dragged before Jesus had done wrong. She had been caught in the very act of adultery. The Pharisees and teachers of the Law were correctly, but selectively, quoting the Mosaic Law, which does call for the death of one caught in adultery. What would Jesus do? Would he have the woman stoned, or would he disobey the Law? Jesus seemed to be backed into a corner.

The spiritual condition of the teachers and Pharisees was truly pathetic as revealed in the passage itself. In verse 6 John says, "They were using the question as a trap in order to have a basis for accusing him." Instead of truly seeking to uphold the Law as they pretended, they were only trying to trap Jesus. They had little or no concern for the woman involved. But Jesus saw the woman herself.

Throughout the Prophets in the Old Testament, the sin of adultery is used to symbolize spiritual bankruptcy. According to the prophets, in departing from their relationship to God, disobeying the Covenant and turning to pagan gods, Israel became a spiritual whore. While claiming a privileged relationship to God, Israel was apostate in their hearts and lives. These accusers of the woman displayed the same spiritual bankruptcy in their treacherous attitude and failure to obey the whole Law they so glibly quoted. While it is true that the penalty for adultery was death, the Pharisees had omitted two other points of the law: 1) that both the woman and the man were to be brought for punishment by eyewitnesses, 2) that there was first to be a warning used, and only after the second offense was there to be punishment.

These men made a mockery of the Law they claimed to live by misusing it for evil purposes and victimizing the woman. Their actions revealed the spiritual poverty that had characterized religious Israel for several hundred years. Correctly reading their twisted use of the Law and the evil in their hearts, Jesus gives the wise answer, "If anyone of you is without sin, let him be the first to throw a stone at her" [John 8:7].

Before we begin to feel superior to these religious leaders, we need to be sobered by this realization: it is just as much a danger today for people in the Body of Christ to become spiritual *adulterers*. While claiming a devotion to Scripture and a zeal for righteousness, like the Pharisees Christian hearts can become cold and indifferent to Jesus. Evil intents and twisted uses of God's Word can usurp our energies and take us far from God.

> **Before we begin to feel superior to these religious leaders, we need to be sobered by this realization: it is just as much a danger today for people in the Body of Christ to become spiritual adulterers.**

Jesus was full of compassion towards the woman. Immediately after answering the woman's accusers, Jesus stooped down and wrote on the ground. Those who had accused the woman begin to leave one at a time. Unlike our wordy attempts to minister, Jesus merely lets God's wisdom do its work, remaining silent. Jesus' words to the woman contain both truth and mercy: "Woman, where are they? Has no one condemned you?" "No one sir," she said. "Then neither do I condemn you," Jesus declared. "Go now, and leave your life of sin'" [John 8:10-11].

Jesus did not endorse or excuse her sin any more than He will excuse ours. Yet in a graphic display of God's compassion and mercy, He pardons her. Just as this woman deserved condemnation, we also deserve to be eternally punished and separated from God's presence, yet we too have received a pardon because of the death of Jesus.

Here Jesus reveals the very heart of the gospel as He embodies and demonstrates the compassion of God. If we want to know what God is like, we need only to look at Jesus.

In our efforts to serve God and be good Christians, it is all too easy to transform the mercy of God into a gospel of performance and condemnation. We think that though we were saved by grace we must maintain God's love through performance. Part of this performance includes self-improvement, and part includes setting sinners straight. We may smugly condemn abortionists, pornographers and other moral offenders while harboring bitterness, resentment and self-righteousness in our hearts.

We think that though we were saved by grace we must maintain God's love through performance.

We are still in need of the mercy of God—forgiveness and restoration. We dare not lose sight of the mercy of God as it is displayed in this account. Jesus stands always ready to minister to us in our sin and need. Just as we have received forgiveness and cleansing when we first put our faith in Jesus, we can receive it daily. Not only will our lives be refreshed and energized, but receiving God's love and mercy will also produce a love and mercy in us for others. We will be able to carry out the ministry of Jesus in the mercy and love of Jesus. One without the other just doesn't work!

LEARNING TO LOVE

Consistent love for other Christians is key to a healthy spiritual life because loving fellowship is God's prescribed environment for growth.

This kind of love is based on commitment to God Himself. To be committed to God is to be committed to His community, the Church. This is not a commitment to the theory of the Church, but to an actual body of other fallible, imperfect people.

Many of us treat church life like immature adolescents. From other Christians we want thrills, constant exhilaration and to have our needs met. When Christian brothers and sisters fall short of our expectations, when they are boring, imperfect and fail to meet our needs for strokes, we pout, turn away and isolate ourselves from them. Jesus calls us to mature commitment of love for His people—the very people in our fellowship!

> **This is not a commitment to the theory of the Church, but to an actual body of other fallible, imperfect people.**

I have many fond memories and warm thoughts about the fellowship I was a part of as a baby Christian. It is true that the dear people who nursed me through Christian babyhood were not perfect. But their cardinal virtue was the fact that they consistently loved and accepted me even as an immature and messy baby Christian!

Without their love and care I might have never made it through this crucial time. Like these kind and patient Christians, we need to learn how to keep people through love. Despite imperfections, sins and irritating habits of other Christians, they belong to Jesus, and they need our love as a healthy climate for growth.

LOVE IN A JAR OF PEANUT BUTTER

Over the years I can't tell you how many times people have very kindly come up to me and said, "You are such a loving man." I've had to smile because for the first ten years of my Christian life that's the number one thing I prayed for. I prayed, "Lord, I don't have any love for anybody but me, and I don't even like me very much!" I realize that if there's any love in me, it's clearly the work of God. It's something that God has produced because I haven't done anything to make it happen, except to pray.

I've said in the past, "If love were peanut butter, my jar is empty all the time." Have you ever tried to dig down and get the last residue of that nutty spread? That's the way my jar feels all the time. Many times I've had to say, "Oh God, fill the jar, here's someone that wants a sandwich!" Do you know that feeling? I'm sure you do, but he fills it all the time. You can read John 15:5 like this, "I am the vine, and you are the branches, if a man remains in me and I in him, he will bear much peanut butter." There's nothing we can do apart from Jesus.

Judas found that out, didn't he? That's whom I think Jesus was referring to in John 15:

"He cuts off every branch in me that bears no fruit. If anyone does not remain in me, he is like a branch that is thrown away and withers. Those branches are picked up, thrown into the fire, and burned. If you remain (abide, live, take your resource) in me and my words remain (abide, live, and take their resource) in you, ask whatever you wish and it will be given to you. This is to my Father's glory that you bear much fruit, showing yourselves to be my disciples" (vv. 2, 6-8).

WALKING IN LOVE

How can we avoid the militant mindset against other believers and embrace others with differing views? It comes down to Paul's admonition: "Accept one another, just as Christ accepted you…" (Romans 15:7). The Church is called to a loving and accepting attitude. That's the ethos I desire for the Vineyard Movement.

Accepting one another in the Body of Christ just as Jesus did with warts and all, with differing viewpoints and argumentative attitudes. How did Christ accept us? Did Christ wait until we were "acceptable," or "eligible" for fellowship before dying for us? No, He adopted us into the family, even before we knew we needed Him. Actually He accepted us while we were still His spiritual enemies. "But God demonstrates his own love for us in this: While were still sinners, Christ died for us" (Romans 5:8). That's the standard of love and acceptance we have as Christians.

You might say, "You mean I'm supposed to accept my brother when he's out of line and when he doesn't even seem to be trying to get along? What about when he's doing all the stuff I hate?" It all comes down to this issue of truth and mercy. In truth, Jesus accepted you at a time when you weren't ready to be accepted. Your life wasn't "in line." You weren't in the place you should have been. The way out of the dilemma is by learning to walk in maturity and love.

LOVE AND COMPASSION: THE BASIS OF JESUS' MINISTRY

In the first few years of our fellowship's existence we often referred to ourselves as the "walking wounded." Many of us had been "pillars" of our former churches—we had taught Sunday School, sat on committees, taught Bible studies, set up chairs for special meetings and done countless other worthwhile activities seeking to serve God. But in the process we had been hurt, bruised, battered and worn out from church life. Ministering to others was difficult if not impossible. In our exhausted state we turned to God and learned to worship, to minister to God. As we began to be healed and revitalized in worship, we then started to have fellowship with each other in our "kinship" groups. As a natural outgrowth of worship and fellowship we saw the need to start ministering to others. God gave us new understanding and clarity about ministry by highlighting the ministry of Jesus while He was on earth.

At the very outset of His ministry Jesus announces in a Nazareth synagogue the nature of His ministry using a passage from Isaiah 61 [Luke 4:18-19].

From this point on Jesus would heal people, cast out their demons, preach and teach, saying, "The Kingdom of God is at hand," or "The Kingdom of God has come upon you." The Kingdom of God in the New Testament means the rule or reign of God. In preaching the gospel to the poor, releasing people from the emotional and spiritual forces that enslaved them, and bringing physical wholeness to those broken and crushed by disease, Jesus was actually expanding God's Kingdom in visible and tangible ways. It is clear what is important to Jesus—liberating people from the traps of Satan and their own sin and bringing them into relationship with God are clearly Jesus' ministry priorities.

This ministry is all based on compassion and the mercy of God. Jesus was the living evidence of God's mercy and compassion on those who were helpless and in need of His love. Matthew 9:35 tells us that Jesus went through all the towns and villages teaching in their synagogues preaching the good news of the kingdom and healing every disease and sickness. Verse 36 states, "When he saw the crowds he had compassion on them, because they were harassed and helpless, like sheep without a shepherd." This compassion also caused Him to give sight to the blind [Matthew 20:29-24], to cleanse the leper [Mark 1:40-41] and to feed the multitudes [Mark 8:1-8]. Today, as the Body of Christ we are to continue to be the vessels of the ministry of compassion and mercy.

Our call is to minister mercy and compassion to the lost, the poor and the sick.

Sharing in the lives of others has given me much joy throughout the years, as well as much heartache personally. But I owe a debt of gratitude for all of the lives I have been a part of through the years. They have given me so much more than I have been able to give to them. Though I have blundered at times, they have been very patient and gracious to me as I continue to have God's love perfected in my life. Mother Teresa has said, "We can do no great things for God, only small things with great love."

How can I say I love Jesus and not respond to Him? His call has always been to deny myself and follow Him. John writes, "This is how we know what love is: Jesus Christ laid down his life for us. And we ought to lay down our lives for our brothers. If anyone has material possession and sees his brother in need but has no pity on him, how can the love of God be in him? Dear children, let us not love with words or tongue but with actions and in truth" [1 John 3:16-18].

The Cost of Commitment

"BIG DECISIONS NEED BIG DIRECTIONS."

"OLD ORDERS ARE STANDING ORDERS UNTIL
YOU GET NEW ORDERS."

I 've been getting saved now for over thirty years. Sure, there was that moment in 1963 when I decided to follow Christ. But that decision has been followed by thousands of daily decisions to keep following. The word "converted" doesn't cover it for me—I need to be salvaged. The plain truth is that I have to get "converted" almost every morning, in one sense. I wake up "unsaved," and I have to decide whom I am going to spend the day for: Jesus or me.

I'm talking about my feelings here. I know I haven't lost my salvation overnight; I am just saying I don't wake up as tuned in to God as I was when I went to sleep. Being a disciple is not easy. It takes daily discipline. It takes more than multiple spiritual experiences with God, although spiritual experience must not be shot down in our lives either. Our ultimate destination in Christ is to arrive found in Him. While we are on the way, He cleans us up as we yield our wills, our plans and ourselves to Him. There are key biblical truths we must embrace after we have made the decision to follow Him. These truths act as the rudders that keep us on course through the River of Life.

AN EARLY LESSON

I hadn't been a Christian more than six weeks, and I loved Sunday school. The guy who had led me to the Lord was teaching a class, and I loved to go to it. One day I was driving to church with my family, and I saw a person with a flat tire. I thought, "Gee, I wish I had time to stop for him, but I've got to get down to the church building and get the chairs arranged for Sunday school." So I went on by and got the chairs arranged for Sunday school, and all the adults came in and sat down in the chairs, but the teacher wasn't there. We waited five, ten, fifteen, twenty-five minutes. The class was only forty-five minutes long. About twenty-five minutes after the hour, he comes in with grease all over his hands. "Forgive me, you all," he said, "I had to stop and help somebody with a flat tire!" That day he taught me one of the greatest lessons I ever learned as a Christian.

Are you hearing me? "I had to stop. A man needed help." We didn't have time for the lesson that morning, but he didn't need to say anything after that. I got on board that day. For the first time I understood the priority of just helping people, whatever the situation. Discipleship requires obedience. In Matthew 21, Jesus says, "Not everyone who says to me 'Lord, Lord' will enter the Kingdom, only those who do the will of the Father in Heaven" (verse 21). Doing is the thing. Faith, James says, is proven by our deeds. Christianity is evidential. At the end of the day, it's all about obedience. It's not enough to say, "Lord, Lord." You've got to act. Not everybody is necessarily called to the "front lines" of work with the poor, but everyone is called to participate.

ONE STEP AT A TIME

From time to time the Lord challenges us to make new commitments. God lets us know that He wants us to give up something we are successful at and begin doing something we do not yet know anything about—maybe something we do not even like.

The simple fact is that the Lord has the right to call us to make any changes and sacrifices He wants. After all, He has loved us before the foundation of the world and purchased us at the price of His own blood. We are not our own. But when God exercises that right, we often go into a tailspin. "Who does God think He is?" We protest. "I've just gotten my life to where I want it, I'm just going in the direction I want to go and now He's telling me I have to do something different."

The economy of the Kingdom of God is quite simple. Every new step into the Kingdom costs us everything we have gained to date.

What do we do? Do we back off, take a vacation from obedience and sacrifice and do our own thing? Do we try to hang on to Jesus while brushing away the cross? Or do we say yes to Jesus and no to our desires, releasing the power of God in our lives?

The economy of the Kingdom of God is quite simple. Every new step into the Kingdom costs us everything we have gained to date. Every time we cross a new threshold, it costs us everything we now have. Every new step may cost us all the reputation and security we have accumulated up to that point. It costs us our life.

A disciple is a follower, an acolyte, a student, an apprentice. A disciple of Jesus is always ready to take the next step with Him. If there is anything that characterizes Christian maturity, it is the willingness to become a beginner again for Jesus Christ. It is the willingness to put our hand in His hand and say, "I'm scared to death, but I'll go with you. You're the Pearl of great price."

MEASURING A DISCIPLE

What does a disciple look like? When I became a Christian at twenty-nine, I was not a good candidate for becoming a disciple of Jesus. For one thing, I was much more familiar with "bar" and "nightclub" life than with church life and etiquette. As a lounge musician I knew well the social dynamics of when a person was "out" or "in" with other patrons or lounge employees. However, I felt totally out of my element in a church service, even referring to the ushers as "bouncers." However, it wasn't long before I had been well-schooled in the "rules" of church life according to my denomination. With an earnest desire to be Jesus' disciple, I determined to meet all the expectations of the leadership of my fellowship.

Over the last several years as a pastor and speaker at many church conferences, I have had the opportunity to closely observe pastors from some thirty denominations. I have spoken at some 400 pastors' conferences. As a result, I have discovered that, without exception, each denomination has its "tests of fellowship." These criteria determine whether a person is really "committed" or not. Among these "discipleship criteria" are these basics:

1. Church attendance: a novice can get by with attending once a week, but a "mature" Christian will surely be in church twice on Sunday and at midweek prayer meeting.

2. Giving: One must tithe [give at least 10%] of his income.

3. Service: A truly committed person is expected to serve the church by working in the Sunday school or at least work with various youth groups.

4. Doctrine: A real disciple will maintain "sound doctrine." (Usually sound doctrine seen through our denominational uniqueness)

5. Practice: One must abstain from going certain places and doing certain things. (Each church has its own list of "Thou shalt not's"-the members will quickly inform new people of their particular list.)

Usually these "tests of fellowship" or "rules of church life" are earnestly believed by members to be the same as true Biblical discipleship. These people can easily be drawn into arguments defending their particular position.

When viewed through the lens of the New Testament, these denominational standards simply do not correspond to Jesus' expectations regarding discipleship. In fact, when Jesus confronted conservative religious people like the Pharisees, he rebuked them for paying such close attention to their manmade interpretations of the Law while ignoring the heart of what it means to be in relationship with God. In contrast to these people's misguided piety, Jesus presents the essence of what it means to be a citizen of the Kingdom of God in his Sermon on the Mount and in the brief but profound summary of the Law, "Love the Lord your God with all your heart, with all your soul and with all your mind....Love your neighbor as yourself" (Matthew 22:37, 39).

In addition to this teaching, Jesus demonstrated discipleship and the Kingdom in action by ministering in compassion and power to people He met, healing their bodies, minds and spirits. Christianity is a personal relationship with Christ in which we involve ourselves first in loving and knowing God and then in showing His love to others in His words and works.

So, how do we measure a disciple? First and foremost, through lives poured out in service. Disciples are willing to do things. We help followers understand that we've been called to lay our lives down as an act of worship (Romans 12:1,2).

I've been privileged to know men and women who have used their own money, some of them going around the world a dozen times, to serve the purposes of God. These people are inspiring, but one thing is for sure: they have learned how to serve at home long before they got on a jet.

Back in 1978 a young man, who later served as the U.S. National Director of Churches, came to me and told me he wanted to go and plant a church. He didn't have a clue what the town he wanted to go to was like, but I could see the fire in his eyes, and I could tell his wife was also committed to doing this thing. I could see energy and leadership in both of them and determined to help them.

First, I made it as hard as I could by giving him tough assignments. "Go down to the hospital and pray for the sick." Do you think the nurses welcomed a twenty-two year old kid who wanted to lay hands on patients? But he got in, and over time people got touched and blessed. Eventually people started showing up at the church. Some of them even got healed in the process. Then I said, "How about starting a small group?" Next thing I know, he's got a flourishing small group, and people are getting saved. He passed every test I gave him. Finally, the Holy Spirit said it was time for him to go. I knew I could send him, not because of what he knew, but because he had demonstrated his commitment through practical service.

The second measurement of disciples is whether church life is at the center of their lives. Loving Christ is only part of the picture. We also need to love what He loves, which is the whole Church. Disciples love the Church because God loves the Church. He doesn't look down from heaven at a Church divided and defeated. He sees a bride preparing herself for marriage to His Son.

The Church is the only thing Jesus is coming back for. If the people who come to our churches get connected with Christ, they may or may not stay. But if they get connected with Christ and with other brothers and sisters in Christ, they'll probably stay, unless the Lord moves them out. They're looking for relationship and identity. They're looking for reality and something that will get them through life.

Many years ago C. Peter Wagner and I traveled to different churches to consult with the Fuller Evangelistic Association. I must have heard Pete say a hundred times, "If I lived in this city, I would come to this church." Every time he said it, he meant it. He loves the Church in all her many-faceted expressions. Pete would sit and cry in the various worship services we attended. I thought he was crying from embarrassment; I finally realized it was joy.

Another way of measuring a disciple is by the way he thinks. Following Jesus should affect our thought patterns. Are you and the people you're training thinking in disciple-ese? The fundamentals of the Gospel become as important to a committed disciple's spiritual life as the heart and lungs are to his physical body.

We want to engender a deep spirituality in our life that rejects facile triumphalism. Disciples realize there will be hard times ahead. The journey we're on is fraught with pain, difficulties and the onslaughts of the enemy. We also learn we can benefit from trials.

He doesn't look down from heaven at a Church divided and defeated. He sees a bride preparing herself for marriage to His Son.

From my reading of the Bible and Church history, Christianity doesn't guarantee heaven here on earth. We're going to heaven, but we may go through hell here.

Maturity does not automatically come with the passage of years. Some of the people we work with may be spiritually much younger than their chronological age. A prayer I pray often is "Lord, let me grow up before I grow old."

SHOW AND TELL

According to Matthew 28:18-20, the Church has been called to go and make disciples. The word from which we translate "disciple," (*mathetes* -- math-ay-TES) means "learner, pupil, or disciple." When we think of a learner or pupil in our Western minds, we usually think of classrooms with desks and students. While that is not bad, it is not what the New Testament means in its use of the word.

Greek pupils or Rabbinic students bound themselves personally to their master and looked for objective teaching, with the aim of themselves becoming a master or a Rabbi. But Jesus' call to discipleship does not mean that a disciple is put in a learning relationship from which he can depart as a master or teacher. Following Jesus as disciple means the unconditional sacrifice of one's whole life (Matthew 10:39; Luke 14:26f; Mark 3:31-35). To be a disciple of Jesus means, in Matthew particularly, to be bound to Jesus and to do God's will (Matthew 12:46-50).

In the Gospel of Matthew, we see Jesus in action as a discipler, or trainer of men. We marvel at the practicality and effectiveness of His way of training. He uses a "show, tell and do" method of training. The entire book of Matthew can be divided into five books. Within each of these books there is both an instructive "tell" section and a narrative "show" section. After the large section of teaching in the first of the book, Jesus takes His disciples on a healing trip in Chapters 8 and 9. These chapters contain no less than nine accounts of miracles; in reaching out to people in need of healing and deliverance, Jesus is "showing" His disciples what the Kingdom is. Then in chapter 10, He commissions them to go and do the same things (Matt. 10:1, 7, 8a).

Jesus' way of training is much like a mother bird who teaches her babies to fly by first allowing them to try their own wings. His goal was to pass on, by example, the words and the works of the Kingdom to people who would put them into action and eventually pass them onto others. The results of Jesus' training can be seen clearly in the book of Acts as we see the disciples of Jesus saying the words of

> **Training, then, is being equipped rather than educated. It is being formed as well as informed.**

the Kingdom and doing the works of the Kingdom just as Jesus did before them. We see them preaching sermons in the power of the Holy Spirit and thousands being converted (Acts 2:14-41). We see them healing the lame and the blind and delivering those tormented by evil spirits. It is also evident that they were passing on the ministry by showing and telling a second generation of disciples like Phillip and Steven.

Training, then, is being equipped rather than educated. It is being formed as well as informed. This is not to say we should be anti-educational. There is a time and place to gain the theory and the theology concerning what we are doing. However, our priority should be training people to know the Words of Jesus and do to the *works* of Jesus.

At the Vineyard church where I pastor, our training is based on forming relationships with those we're training and using this "show-and-tell" model of training. For instance, when I train someone:

- I model it (for example, praying for the sick)
- I continue to model it with the trainee watching
- I get the trainee to "do" as I interact with him
- I leave him/her doing it and tell them to check back with me
- I instruct him/her to model for someone else

This is exactly how I learned to witness and how thousands have learned to pray for others.

Maturing in Christ

"I WANT TO GROW UP BEFORE I GROW OLD"

Too often Christians focus on gifts—natural and supernatural—and ignore character. But this bypasses a fundamental principle of the Christian life: gifts and abilities, no matter how magnificent, are either limited or enhanced by character.

I find this phenomenon to be very widespread among Christians. In fact, it was a great stumbling block to my coming into the power of the Holy Spirit. One of the main reasons I used to resist speaking in tongues was that I didn't like a lot of the tongue-speakers I had met!

Gifts are to character as adornments are to a body. Beautiful adornments, such as jewelry and fine clothing, look good on a beautiful body. But when the body has been neglected and has itself become unattractive, you can do almost anything to it—jewel it, perfume it, deck it out in gorgeous clothes—and it still doesn't look right.

So it is with spiritual gifts. They are to be adornments to a well-formed character, which is the foundation for properly displaying them. We are to seek the fruit of the Spirit as a precursor to seeking the gifts of the Spirit. An important characteristic of fruit is that it grows, going through a process of development that culminates into maturity. Fruit doesn't grow to maturity in one day; it goes through a process of development in which both internal factors (its genetic makeup) and external factors (water, soil, temperature) combine to create maturity.

As Christians we go through a process of character formation in which the fruit of the Spirit grows to maturity in us. With the Holy Spirit living in us, we have the "genetic makeup" to reflect God's nature. But initial conversion does not ensure Christian maturity. We must be willing to submit patiently to and cooperate aggressively with the process of discipleship, understanding that there are no shortcuts to maturity.

Many times we are impatient with this process, and we seek to cut it short. I often find people seeking to achieve maturity through either magic or structure. These people are on to something real. They are seeking happiness and fulfillment in their Christian lives. But they have not yet learned to equate that fulfillment with the completion of a process of growth.

Some of them want to have the "magic wand of prayer" waved over them, as though by laying hands on them and uttering the right combination of syllables we could transform them into spiritual super saints, able to leap tall problems in a single bound. Others come to the spiritual life seeking structure, believing that the right set of spiritual disciplines, methods and techniques will catapult them into spiritual maturity.

It is important to realize that both prayer and structure do play important roles in the process of growth. But neither is complete in itself. Many people experience great liberation and forward momentum as a result of prayer ministry, but we cannot simply "pray in" complete and total Christian maturity.

Spiritual disciplines and methods can move us ahead a great deal. But they can be somewhat deceptive. A new technique or approach will often seem fabulously effective for a while. But once the novelty wears off, it remains effective only as we continue to pursue it patiently over a long period of time.

Anyone who has ever gone on a diet will be familiar with the phenomenon: for the first few days weight loss is rapid and relatively effortless. Then we reach a plateau, and progress toward our weight goal comes more slowly.

I have seen this principle played out in my own spiritual life recently. My wife Carol and I sensed the Lord calling us to more regular and vigorous intercessory prayer on behalf of the churches we are connected with. The first few months were glorious. Every morning we rose early and met with God. It was dynamic and exciting! I was beginning to suspect that I just might be one of the best pray-ers in the entire Body of Christ.

But it didn't take too long before it felt more like drudgery. The excuses came: I can't get up on time; I can't stay awake once I do get up. Something inside me seems to scream, "This is stupid! God may not even be awake yet! Why am I dragging myself out of bed like this?" Some mornings it feels as though all I'm doing is sitting in a chair and dribbling coffee into my beard. If I were counting on structure to move my spiritual life ahead, I'd have given up on this particular practice long ago.

We need to come to grips with the reality that there are no shortcuts. Growth in character is a process, one that happens one day at a time, one step at a time.

SPIRITUAL ACUMEN

When we have committed to the Lord in an act of surrender, we begin the process of life in Christ. We spend the rest of our years trying to please Him and often we find ourselves measuring our progress. Sometimes we make the mistake of evaluating ourselves based on the gifts He gives us.

The Lord showed me awhile back that there is a difference between our spiritual giftedness and our spiritual acumen. Although we may be endowed with various gifts of the Spirit such as tongues, prophesying, healing and deliverance, we may have to grow in other dimensions of our faith. I define spiritual acumen as the measurement of how much a Spirit-filled person acts on what he or she believes.

The book of James exhorts us to be doers of the Word. The accumulation of what you do determines your spiritual acumen.

"Do not merely listen to the Word, and so deceive yourselves. Do what it says. Anyone who listens to the Word, but does not do what it says is like a man who looks at his face in the mirror and after looking at himself goes away and immediately forgets what he looks like" (James 1:22-24).

A LIFE THAT PLEASES JESUS

What do you think of when you hear terms like spiritual growth, mature faith, and growing closer to God? Many of us struggle with vague feelings of guilt, of falling short of some indefinite or uncertain standard. Sources of that standard may differ for each of us: parents, educators, peers, the media, our conscience and so on.

People who are seeking God are aware of an even higher standard for growth and maturity that is found in the pages of Scripture. Frequently, we struggle with guilt and discouragement because no matter how hard we try, we can't measure up to God's standards. We always seem to fall short of the righteousness and love of God, even when we give it our best shot. We try following good rules, obeying sure principles and conforming to high moral standards of behavior. But is this kind of frustrating—and impossible—effort truly the essence of growth and change? God's ways are always different from the world's ways and are always much more rewarding.

One of the most famous passages in the Bible begins, "For God so loved the world, that He gave his one and only Son, that whoever believes in Him shall not perish but have eternal life." It continues, however, with a lesser-known insight into the character of the Father: "...for God did not send his Son into the world to condemn the world, but to save the world through him. Whoever believes in him is not condemned, but whoever does not believe stands condemned already because he has not believed in the name of God's one and only Son" (John 3:16-18).

I've been told I have a pretty good sense of humor. Often I find myself laughing at something I have done that did not turn out like I had expected. Humor really is good medicine. Sometimes I think we Christians take ourselves too seriously; maybe we should all laugh a little more.

But there is one thing I am very serious about: living a life that pleases Jesus. I am so serious about it that when I was first saved, if a mature Christian had told me the way to really please God and grow spiritually was to perform some death-defying feat, I just might have done it.

Thankfully, I was never asked to do anything so dangerous, but I was given the impression that to really please God I should be a good church member—which included regular attendance (twice weekly), giving, working in the Sunday school, adherence to our denominational creed and the ability to smile and look spiritual on Sunday at church. I worked hard to meet these criteria, and many of them were beneficial to me. Yet I consistently failed to see the maturity and fruitfulness that others implied would surely come if I did these things.

I have since realized that these criteria are common to most churches, and they do not necessarily produce the quick maturity and fruitfulness many of us are seeking. In fact, if we reduce Christianity to these things alone, we might totally miss the life and relationship with God that He intends for us! It is so easy for us to think of Christian faith as a religion or an organization to which we belong. The reality is that God desires a growing and dynamic relationship with us that expresses itself in love and service to others.

Walking with Jesus and serving Him are serious issues.

WHAT IS PERFECTION?

Early in Philippians 3, the apostle Paul is warning the church in Philippi about opponents—he refers to them as dogs!—who are "mutilators of the flesh" (Philippians 3:2). These people, called Judaizers in Paul's letter to the Galatians, were teaching the necessity of religious works to be saved, in this case, circumcision. Paul strongly objected, arguing that we are saved through faith, drawn by God's grace. He denies that he, or any of us, has already reached a state of perfection in our faith.

A word needs to be said here concerning perfection. Perfection is Paul's goal; as long as he is on earth, he said, he will strive to reach that goal (See Philippians 3:14). But what does Paul mean by perfection? The person who has "been made perfect" (Philippians 3:12) is fully-grown, mature, complete, adult—not flawlessly perfect. Perfection describes a quality relationship with God, one marked by habitual intimacy and dependence on His grace.

In fact, the Greek word translated "perfect" in Philippians 3:12 is translated "mature" in Philippians 3:15 in the New International Version. The mature person, then, is one who has made reasonable progress in his or her spiritual growth, by placing his or her faith in the finished work of Jesus Christ:

"I want to know Christ and the power of His resurrection and the fellowship of sharing in His sufferings, becoming like Him in his death, and so, somehow, to attain to the resurrection from the dead" (Philippians 3:10, 11).

POWER POINTS

The process of spiritual growth is punctuated by certain crucial moments that I call power points. These power points are the spaces where core Christian truths intersect with our lives. If we follow them well, they change the direction of our lives and direct us toward increasing maturity.

They change the direction of our lives by first changing us. They change the way we think about God, ourselves and the people around us. They also change the way we live. At each point we become a little more like Jesus, reflecting some new aspect of His character in our character and actions.

I use the term power points because they are or can be "eureka moments" when we know—really know—some key truth of the Christian life. These are points in time in which understanding and experience come together. Eureka means an exclamation of triumphant achievement, equivalent to "I've got it! I've mastered it! I've understood it!" That's what a power point is—an "I've got it!" time in our relationship with God.

Power points are more than the objective markers along the path of spiritual growth; they are experiences of God's truth that boost us along, catapulting us toward maturity. Power points raise our vision and sense of calling. Elevated vision in turn creates an expectant, highly motivated environment. When we experience power points, we want to take on new spiritual challenges, and as a result, we grow.

Power points are rooted in objective truth about God, which keeps us on a sure path toward maturity. They are like the pitons, or metal spikes, that mountain climbers rely on for safety when they scale steep, rocky cliffs. As the climbers move up the mountain, they plant the pitons firmly in rock. The lead climber passes the rope through them. The rope is attached to the climber below as well as the lead climber. Should the lead climber fall off the cliff, he will remain attached to the piton and climber below, thus not falling to his death. With this system (called belaying), climbers can never fall too far from where they last planted a piton.

Knowing Jesus puts us on the mountain, along the path to maturity. But to grow, we need to continue climbing and planting pitons. It is good to know, though, that if we slip, the last piton is always there. Jesus Himself is the climber below holding the rope.

THE DEEPER LIFE

I was never any good at family devotions. I read children's Bible stories to my kids, but they usually got bored. Booklets and games didn't do it either. I never fit the mold of a great family devotions leader. But I lived a devoted life. My wife Carol and I led friends to Christ in our living room. We served meals, loaned money and taught Bible studies in our home.

Our kids watched and listened. They remember a number of instances that served to form their understanding of the Christian life. In their thirties they all indicated to me, using different language, that three things made it possible for them to be believers. First, Carol and I were always the same in public and private. Secondly, we always made room for them in whatever we were doing. Finally, Carol and I were almost always together on our various positions or opinions in our household. This seemed to give the family some stability.

They also remember the stories I told from my travels as a Christian leader. One of their favorites is about the time I cast out demons while eating a bag of potato chips. They thought it was funny. I didn't know if you were supposed to do that or not; chips and demons aren't mentioned together in the Bible. In any case, these stories served to reinforce the practices and principles of our family's spiritual framework. Ordinary life and spiritual activities intersected in our home.

Today for many people it's in vogue to focus on acquiring supernatural experiences—you know, those exciting manifestations of God's power. However, I want to remind these folks that we must value the ordinary expressions of our faith as well. Don't get me wrong, I'm all for experiences with God. I love the sense of His touch and presence. But I also love the fullness of the ordinary Christian life. Some call it the deeper life. I call it the only life.

WHAT DOES GOD SAY ABOUT YOUR MONEY?

"COMMITMENT IS SPELLED: M.O.N.E.Y"

Hebrews 13:5 says, "Keep your lives free from the love of money and be content with what you have…" Thousands of Christians who would never turn to adultery or sexual immorality easily become involved in the love of money. Our culture measures success and even individual worth in terms of the size of one's income or bank account and by the material possessions he has. Affluence and materialism then become major objects of worship for us; they become what we serve and what we strive for. The worship of money, success and possessions is a major form of idolatry in our society today. Jesus gave this warning to his followers: "You cannot serve God and money" (Matthew 6:24b).

And yet today many Christians and Christian leaders have been neutralized by the love of money and materialism. The homage paid to affluence becomes a burden that saps our energy as well as our love for God and other people. Through repentance and the cleansing of forgiveness, we can rid ourselves of this burden and begin to let God transform our value system. Like Jesus and Paul, we can learn to be content with what we have, living modestly in order that we may give liberally.

WHAT YOU NEED TO KNOW ABOUT YOUR MONEY

Back in 1987, I took a look at my congregation and drew a conclusion: our church, the Anaheim Vineyard, was deficient in many ways. We had a worldwide visibility, but we were hurting in many respects. We had lagged in our Bible teaching, in ministry to the lost and poor, in prayers and in financial giving, especially tithing. These were but four of eight areas in which we needed to grow as a church.

What was the problem? It turned out to be me! I simply had not done my job with the people. I had been so busy working for spiritual renewal in other countries that I hadn't provided the leadership needed at home. So I called the congregation's key leaders together and shared our new emphases and what we were going to do about them. One of them was on financial stewardship.

Why had I avoided speaking directly to so many issues about money that Jesus so frequently and pointedly talked about? Eventually I admitted to myself that I had fallen into the trap of over-reacting to the false teachings of many "health and wealth" televangelists and Christian empire builders. In other words, I had shirked my responsibility to bring the full counsel of God's Word to one of the most sensitive areas in the lives of many Christians.

I don't think I'm alone in my failing. I've talked with many pastors who are so turned off by the self-serving and manipulative techniques of a few highly visible Christian leaders that they are reluctant to preach about money. And a few members of their churches don't want them to teach about a subject that they believe is none of their pastor's business!

But are people's finances really none of the pastor's business? Jesus didn't think so. Twelve of his thirty-eight parables had to do with money, as did one-sixth of the Gospels of Matthew, Mark and Luke. It is now very clear to me that pastors have a responsibility to preach and teach about money, for Christians cannot grow to maturity until their hearts and minds are conformed to Scripture regarding their use of money.

"If a person gets his/her attitude toward money straight," Billy Graham once remarked, "it will help straighten out almost every other area in his/her life."

TWO CONVERSIONS

Martin Luther understood this all too well. He said, "Every Christian needs two conversions, one for his soul and the other for his pocketbook." For this to happen we must preach with passion and conviction not in any way holding back those tough portions in Scripture that may offend some members in the congregation. Take a look at some of these hard sayings of Jesus:

"If you want to be perfect, go, sell your possessions and give them to the poor, and you will have treasure in heaven. Then come, and follow me" (Matthew 19:21).

"Sell your possessions and give to the poor. Provide purses for yourselves

that will not wear out, a treasure in heaven that will not be exhausted, where no thief comes near and no moth destroys" (Luke 12:33).

"Any of you who does not give up everything he has cannot be my disciple" (Luke 14:33).

Jesus presents a consistently negative understanding of material wealth. Paul paints a similar picture, warning leaders that wealth has a narcotic effect on believers, capable of bringing ruin to their faith:

"People who want to get rich fall into temptation and a trap and also into many foolish and harmful desires that plunge men into ruin and destruction. For the love of money is a root of all kinds of evil. Some people, eager for money have wandered from the faith and pierced themselves with many griefs...Command those who are rich in this present world not to be arrogant nor to put their hope in wealth which is so uncertain, but to put their hope in God, who richly provides us with everything for our enjoyment (1 Timothy 6:9-10, 17).

There's no question here in Paul's mind that it is necessary for us as believers to hear warnings and instructions on money. Paul's instruction that he gives to young Timothy, the pastor of the church in Ephesus, was that he be forceful and direct, not mincing words when talking about money. He didn't say, "Suggest to those who are rich..." or, "Gently remind those who are rich..." Paul said, "Command..." Therefore, there are reasons why we need to take money so seriously and with caution. We need to hear what God is saying, so we can be guided and understand correctly instead of taking offense when the pastor gets up to share on finances.

OWNERSHIP

Just a few weeks ago a pastor in our church met with a young man who admitted that until two years ago, he gave little money to the Lord's work. "But I didn't know any better," he said. "I was ignorant. Then pastor John started teaching from the Bible about money, and I learned what God expects from us."

It isn't enough merely to preach to people's hearts; as a pastor, I must also convert their thinking. I believe the most fundamental issue in Scripture on finances is ownership. The question is: who owns our possessions?

On numerous occasions, Jesus used parables to teach basic truths about the Kingdom of God. Several of the parables describe a king or merchant entrusting his possessions to servants, leaving the country for a time, then returning home to find out how the servants have behaved. For example, in the parable of the Talents, a man left three of his servants large amounts of money (talents) and then went on a journey (Matthew 25:14-30). The first two servants invested their master's talents wisely and doubled his money. Upon his return, the master praised them and invited them to share in his happiness.

> **It isn't enough merely to preach to people's hearts; as a pastor, I must also convert their thinking.**

The third servant, however, hid the master's money and earned nothing in his absence. The master was angry with him. The parable of the Talents found in Matthew 25, which reinforces Christ's exhortation that we be watchful in view of the unknown hour of His return, teaches that all we have is owned by God: eternal life, family, our next breath and our material possessions. The idea that we possess anything is a deception. Both the rich and the poor die, and they each leave this world as they came into it: naked.

Psalm 49:10 says, "For all can see that wise men die; the foolish and the senseless alike perish and leave their wealth to others."

1 Timothy 6:7 says, "For we brought nothing into the world, and we can take nothing out of it."

But like the servants in the parable of the Talents, we are entrusted with much. We are stewards of God's possessions. Stewards manage another's property. They are accountable to fulfill the wishes of the owner. We have been redeemed at the cross, and our entire lives were purchased with the precious blood of Christ. He now rightfully possesses the title deed to our souls and bodies, our aspirations and bank accounts. Unless you realize this as a believer, that God is the owner of everything in your life, then every teaching you hear on finances is in vain.

Money is a critical issue, the critical issue for many Christians because it exerts such a powerful pull on their hearts. In the Sermon on the Mount, Jesus spoke directly to the rivalry between money and heaven. First, He asserted, to use a contemporary idiom, that "he who dies with the most toys doesn't win": "Do not store up for yourselves treasures on earth, where moth and rust destroy, and where thieves break in and steal. But store up for yourselves treasures in heaven, where moth and rust do not destroy, and where thieves do not break in and steal" (Matthew 6:19-20).

Woody Allen once remarked, "Money is better than poverty, if only for financial reasons." But what are those financial reasons? The world says that money buys security, freedom, power, identity, pleasure and happiness. In effect, Jesus says, "That may be true, but only for the moment. A day is coming when you can't take it with you." Money can't make anyone rich in the things that count for eternity. Nothing of God's is obtainable by money.

When Simon saw that the Spirit was given at the laying on of the Apostles' hands, he offered them money and said, "Give me also this ability that everyone on whom I lay my hands may receive the Holy Spirit."

Peter answered, "May your money perish with you, because you thought you could buy the gift of God with money! You have no part or share in this ministry, because your heart is not right before God. Repent of this wickedness and pray to the Lord. Perhaps he will forgive you for having such a thought in your heart" (Acts 8:18-24).

In the Sermon on the Mount, Jesus preached to people's hearts, and He wanted His audience to understand money's corrupting effects: "For where your treasure is, there your heart will be also" (Matthew 6:21). Money promises us much, but it demands even more. "Give me your heart," it says, "and I will save you." Its promises are without question among the greatest of Satan's lies.

Money is a jealous god. It demands that we love it exclusively. "No one can serve two masters," Jesus concluded in this section of the Sermon on the Mount. "Either he will hate the one and love the other, or he will be devoted to the one and despise the other. You cannot serve both God and money" (Matthew 6:24).

This is why one of the primary tasks of the pastor, when it comes to the teaching of money, is to convert people's attitudes. Once their hearts are won, their practices will soon follow.

A MAJOR BARRIER

Acknowledging that we are merely stewards of God's property means that we must manage according to His direction. And He has clearly provided us direction for financial management in His Word, the Bible. There are some things I would like to mention that I believe are critical issues about finances that most people would rather avoid hearing or pastors would rather avoid teaching, but which we must hear and teach the congregations so we can experience true financial freedom.

It is very important to be wise when it comes to money. The truth is we must know and be aware that riches can be deceitful. It's important to know how much money can be a major barrier to entering the Kingdom of God. We live in a society in which money is the primary, and for many people the only, measure of personal worth. This is, of course, an absolute lie from the enemy. Our value is found in Christ and His work on the cross.

"Jesus looked around and said to His disciples, 'How hard is it for the rich to enter the kingdom of God!' The disciples were amazed at his words, but Jesus said it again, 'Children, how hard it is to enter the kingdom of God! It is easier for a camel to go through the eye of a needle than for a rich man to enter the kingdom of God.' The disciples were even more amazed and said to each other, 'Who then can be saved?'" (Mark 10:23-26).

E.M. Bounds, reflecting on the deceitfulness of riches, said, "Few men get rich with clean hands. Fewer still get rich with religious hands.

Fewer still hold on to their riches and hold on to Christ with a strong grasp at the same time."

WISE INVESTMENT POLICIES:

Make all you can. We must encourage ourselves daily and also those around us to develop a wise investment policy. John Wesley summed up the Biblical teaching on this point in one sentence: "Make all you can, save all you can." Let's take a closer look at this truth.

"Make all you can." Scripture is full of advice and admonition on how to go about making all you can. It usually comes down to diligence and integrity: Proverbs 14:23 says, "All hard work brings a profit, but mere talk leads only to poverty." Jeremiah 17:11 teaches, "Like a partridge that hatches eggs it did not lay is the man who gains riches by unjust means. When his life is half gone, they will desert him, and in the end he will prove to be a fool."

Our society encourages us to make all we can, but not necessarily in the way that Scripture tells us to go about it, which is by hard work and wise investing—cut corners, look for "get rich quick" schemes, cheat, steal and get away with anything you can. I've found especially that we can't remind our young people too much about diligence and integrity because they are profoundly influenced by the world's propaganda when it comes to money-making.

Save all you can. In Scripture it leaves no doubt that as Christians we are to save:

"Go to the ant, you sluggard; consider its ways and be wise! It has no commander, no overseer or ruler, yet it stores its provisions in summer and gathers its food at harvest" (Proverbs 6:6).
"In the house of the wise are stores of choice food and oil, but a foolish man devours all he has" (Proverbs 21:20).

People who save must resist Western cultural values that encourage us to live for today, have it all now and live beyond our means (Luke

12:15). I've discovered that before people can save, they must learn from how those that lead them live and teach. We need to learn how to control our spending, which involves three things:

1. We can't save if we owe others our future paychecks. Living debt free is one of the keys to discipleship, for "the borrower is servant to the lender (Proverbs 22:7). When we build up consumer debt, we become slaves to those we owe, limiting our options to serve God fully.

2. People who live simply know the dangers of wealth and have learned to be content with what they have. When you receive a raise in your salary or unexpected inheritances, do you ask yourself, "What is the minimum I can live on so I can save and invest the maximum into the Kingdom of God?" (Proverbs 30:7-9; Luke 3:14)

3. It's most important to save money for emergencies, retirement and our children's education. Proverbs 13:22 says, "A good man leaves an inheritance for his children's children." It isn't always possible to put aside adequate sums of money for these needs, but God will honor the small amount that we save, causing it to grow and making up for any lack.

Give all you can. Why is it so important to invest our money wisely? The world's motivation for investing is the accumulation of wealth for the purposes of personal power, pleasure and security. In the Kingdom, we invest with a different goal in mind: that we may honor God (1 Corinthians 10:31). If all we have is a gift from God, the only wise investment is one that God approves of.

"For who makes you different than anyone else? What do you have that you did not receive? And if you did receive it, why do you boast as though you did not?" (1 Corinthians 4:7).

So where does God tell us to first invest His money?: In the Kingdom of God, with tithes and offerings (which are sacrifices beyond our tithes). Formally, I taught that a tithe was not necessarily ten percent. But now I am convinced from Scripture that it is at least that, and that it should be given to the local church.

Christians need to understand, from the Bible, their responsibility to give generously to God's work. God has entrusted the Church with much. If you obey God's directives, I guarantee you'll receive an eternal return on your investment, "where neither moth nor rust consumes and where thieves do not break in and steal."

TEACH US TO PRAY

"OH GOD, OH GOD, OH GOD"

W Where does prayer begin? Certainly, it begins with an understanding of God. Who God is and what He does is of paramount importance in considering prayer. How a person prays discloses what he believes about God. What a person believes about God will determine how he/she prays. Our opinion of who God is will determine how we interact with Him in prayer. Petitions, which one would ask of God, are determined by a thorough understanding of His nature and character. This understanding will define what one asks Him to do.

Understanding the nature of God will help us in our petitions to Him. God is a gentle, loving and kind Father, and He desires what is best for His children. If we accept these attestations of God, we will interact accordingly. Sometimes we can see what a person thinks of God by the way he/she interacts with Him. In the Old Testament, there are some prayers that have the ring of bargaining with God. Jacob made this vow to God, "If God be with me and will watch over me on this journey I am taking and will give me food to eat and clothes to wear that I return safely to my father's house, then the Lord will be my God" (Genesis 28:20-21). The character of Jacob has not been totally altered in his encounter with God (28:10-19).

Jacob had met God personally for the first time, and it had shaken him to his very core, yet nothing seemed to change. He was unable to prevent himself from striking a bargain with God, in effect saying that he would keep his end of the bargain if God would keep His. Sound familiar? I believe we do the very same thing that Jacob did. The reason is that, like Jacob, we do not possess a correct concept of the nature of God: God really does want the best for us.

OUR GOD HAS THE POWER TO ACT

It seems imperative that we must know and believe that when we ask God for something, He has the power to bring about the answer. Throughout the Bible and particularly in the New Testament, we see this idea concerning God's power and willingness to act affirmed. Jesus declares, "All things are possible with God" (Mark 10-27b). Paul tells the people of Asia, "Now to Him who is able to do immeasurably more than all we ask or imagine, according to His power that is at work within us, to Him be the glory in the church and in Christ Jesus throughout all generations, for ever and ever! Amen" (Ephesians 3:20-21).

Of what real benefit is there to continue asking one for something if we believe He is impotent and unable to deliver? The believers in the New Testament believed that God was able to bring about the answer to their requests, (see Acts 4) and as a result, the building was shaken and boldness was given.

CAUSE AND EFFECT PRAYER

One of the greatest problems we face in praying is holding on to the tension that God can and will do what He wants, while at the same time feeling that our prayers will make a difference of some kind and perhaps influence God to act on our behalf.

Because of this tension, some fatalists simply will not pray believing that it will not make any difference. It is apparent to me that a person must believe that God is responsive to human influence if prayer is to occur in his life.

The New Testament indicates that prayer does get a response from God. In Matthew, we are told to "Ask, and it will be given to you" (Matthew 7:7). There is an implication of cause and effect between asking God and receiving from God; a failure to ask God can result in a failure to receive, while asking will allow for receiving. Furthermore, James tells us, "When you ask, you do not receive because you ask with the wrong motives" (James 4:3). It behooves us then to learn to ask, believing and letting God examine and purify our motives so that we can become more effective in prayer.

Sometimes God initiates His sovereign plan in our lives and discloses it to us in the aftermath of prayer. In the story of Cornelius and Peter, both are praying at two different places and two different times. In fact, it is while at prayer that Cornelius is visited in a vision by an angel. While Peter was praying, he was put into trance by the Spirit, and an incredible scenario was acted out before him teaching him a profound truth. Prayer is seen as playing a vital part in the action of God bringing the two together (see Acts 10).

The New Testament affirms that God does answer the prayers of His people. The exact way in which these prayers affect God is nowhere discussed; however, personalities in Scripture such as Abraham, David, Jacob, Job, Jesus and Paul pray on numerous

> God responsively interacted with them in a way that shows an incredible willingness on His part to work with those whom He has chosen to have relationship.

occasions, and Scripture demonstrates God responsively interacted with them in a way that shows an incredible willingness on His part to work with those whom He has chosen to have relationship.

UNDERSTANDING OUR NEED FOR HELP

Because of Adam's fall, we find ourselves born into a fallen and sinful state, unable to help ourselves. God, through the work of Jesus, has provided a way for us to move from one state to another. We have access through the Christ-Event by which we can, in a spiritual sense, move from this Present Evil Age into the Age to Come. While still living and being controlled by one Age, we have the distinct advantage of being able to request assistance from the other Age. We can communicate with the God of all Ages! That is prayer!

As we see in Romans 8:26-27, the Holy Spirit helps us in our weakness. As it is defined, weakness surely has the primary meaning of not knowing what to pray, but it also shows the stuff of which we are made. There is no place in Scripture that we can find a doctrine of man's self-sufficiency. Left to ourselves, we are easy prey for the evil one. If we really see that we are in this condition, we certainly will want prayer to be a constant practice in our lives.

When we understand that God is a personal, powerful, imminent, susceptible influence, and that we are weak and we need His help, we will begin seeing the value of prayer and its practice in our lives.

TWO DIVINE INTERCESSORS

I don't know if you are like me, but I have struggled with the subject of prayer since I became a Christian. Several people along the way have attempted to instruct and give me understanding concerning this subject. I have followed a few models, which were developed to disciple me to pray. All of that has been helpful, but I still find that after years of being a Christian, prayer is just hard work. It begins with a diligence and discipline to which many of us are reluctant to commit. However, as one pastor said, "Prayer is probably the highest calling that a person can receive. After all, we are joining in a communication that has gone on forever between the Father, the Son and the Holy Spirit." Prayer then is one of the most important aspects of our growth as Christians.

The children of God have two divine intercessors: Jesus is their intercessor in the courts of heaven (Romans 8:34; Hebrews 7:25), and the Holy Spirit is their intercessor in their midst.

JESUS, OUR INTERCESSOR

The promise of continuance is found in Scripture. There we are told that the prayer of intercession for believers would be an on-going ministry of Jesus. In the Romans 8:34 and Hebrews 7:25 passages, the word, "intercede" (*entunchano*) is used, and in both cases the word is in the present tense, indicating continuance. It has a range of definitions from "to light upon," "converse with," to "appeal to." The English word, "intercede," is defined as "to intervene between parties with a view to reconciling differences." In Scripture the word can mean to plead "for" or "against."

There are two usages of the latter. Acts 25:24 shows the Jewish community asking Festus to execute Paul. Paul in Romans 11:2 uses the word to show Elijah's position as he "appealed to God against Israel" (1 Kings 19:10-18). The other passages we are dealing with here show the parties involved in the act of intercession as being in the "for" mode.

Beginning with John 17:6, we see the intercession of Jesus for His disciples. Jesus prayed on many occasions in the New Testament and for differing reasons. His prayer in John 17 is a useful example of His intercession for His disciples. It provides for us in concrete form what may be occurring at the right hand of the Father as Jesus continues to intercede for His whole Body today.

There are no words with which we can adequately communicate the pathos and tenderness of the prayer in John 17. At best, we can grapple with some of our own feelings which occur as we pray concerning others, thereby gaining insight into Jesus' state of mind and heart.

This prayer is based on the conviction stated in 16:33, namely that Jesus has overcome the world and that He had turned His face toward the cross. In this prayer, Jesus' mood was that of hope and faith, not desperation. It is difficult to divide this prayer for study purposes because it forms a unit. There is, however, a movement which seems easy to discern when looking at it as a whole: 1) Jesus prayed about His own glorification (17:1-5); 2) He prayed for His disciples (17:6-19); 3) And Jesus prayed for all who will believe through their ministry (17:20-26).

PRAYER OF GLORIFICATION

The prayer for glorification is found in John 17:1-5. These verses are often used by Bible teachers to show the necessity of praying for one another when placed in difficult circumstances. While it may include such an interpretation, it appears that what Jesus is really praying for is that the Father's will may be done in Him.

Lifting one's eyes toward heaven was an accepted posture for prayer (John 11:41; Mark 7:34). Sometimes one who prayed would prostrate himself in order to adopt an especially humble place of earnest petition. The address of "Father" is the address of a child to a parent. Jesus says that the appointed time had come. To those who mock, the cross appears as an instrument of death and shame, but to Jesus, it was the means for bringing all glory to God the Father and providing eternal life for all men. In verse 3, Jesus gives us a definition of eternal life as He says that eternal life is to know God. Therefore, it surely is valid to understand that Jesus had in mind an ever-increasing knowledge and not something that is given in completeness once for all.

The declaration in verse 5 is that Jesus had finished His work on earth that He had been sent to do. He had completed His task and in the process brought glory to the Father. The work that He did was given to Him by the Father; however, the initiative is seen as resting with the Father. There seems to be a discernable pattern in these first few verses. After beginning His prayer with the intimacy of a father-child relationship, He then petitions the Father, and then proceeds with reasons why this petition should be granted. This is not necessarily a formula for prayer, but it is an indication that Jesus was first and foremost intimate with the Father. Second, that He was accustomed to asking for things and understood the basis to which these things ought to be granted. As Christians we need to be fully cognizant of this basis for prayer.

PRAYER FOR THE DISCIPLES

The prayer of Jesus for His disciples in John 17:6-19 shows us that prayer is a communication between two parties. There is a conversation, simple yet very profound. Interspersed in the conversation Jesus is having with the Father are several requests. The first of these comes at verse 9 where He told the Father that He was praying for the disciples who had been given to Him. His prayer was that while they were in the world God would protect them by the power of His name. Two things can be meant by this last statement:

1) That God should protect them according to His duty as Father. The word "power" in the NIV is not in the Greek text. It appears to be added to give a fuller explanation of the word translated "protect."

2) That God should keep them in a place of security to keep them safe. This one is preferable in view of verse 12, but both could be intended.

The second request is a clarification of the first. In verse 15, Jesus asks the Father to protect His disciples from the evil one. This is certainly an indisputable allusion to the so-called Lord's Prayer and allows one to see this prayer of Jesus with a Kingdom perspective. The third request of Jesus is for the Father to "…Sanctify them by the truth: your Word is truth." Sanctify here has the meaning of consecration (to be set apart).

The request is for the Father to bring them into the sphere of the sacred, and dedicate them to holy use.

THE SPIRIT, OUR INTERCESSOR

I grew up in the Midwest, and one of my favorite rooms was the kitchen. When close family friends and relatives came to visit, the kitchen was the place the family would go. When God spoke to me about starting what now is called the Vineyard, I asked Him what kind of fellowship it would be. He answered by giving me a picture of the kitchen where the intimate fellowship of my family took place. We would not worship him in the parlor, which had its formality, but in the kitchen, which had its intimacy.

It is easy to maintain a family setting when you are only twenty strong; however, it's a little harder when you are 200, and the real test comes when you hit several

> **We would not worship him in the parlor, which had its formality, but in the kitchen, which had its intimacy.**

thousand. Our growth has put our style to the test. This is one of the reasons that in the Vineyard we believe and encourage people to become involved in small groups. It is in this arena that we can remain family.

The second thing that God spoke to me about during that period of time was the issue of praying in the Spirit. The church that I had been a part of did not have a belief system which would allow them to believe in, much less practice, speaking in tongues.

My wife began praying in the Spirit at the conclusion of a dream in which she was delivering a seven-point sermon against speaking in tongues, and on the seventh and final point, she woke up speaking in tongues. God does have a wonderful sense of humor!

We then had the difficult task of informing our friends. They were blown away by the whole idea. During the next few years, I developed a negative defensive language system trying to explain what had happened to me. Praying in the Spirit is now an essential part of my spiritual life.

(See Appendix A for answers to two questions: "What is praying in the Spirit?" and "Who can pray in the Spirit?")

There is no certain way of establishing whether God endowed the people of the Old Testament with such a gracelet. Prayer in the Spirit, however, appears to be heartfelt communication toward God. Here are a few examples where this idea is expressed.

Psalm 42:4 says, "These things I remember as I pour out my soul." Psalm 62:8 says, "Pour out your heart to Him." And Lamentations 2:19 states, "Pour out your heart like water in the presence of the Lord."

All three of these texts are set in Hebrew poetry and must be read with the emotion with which they were penned.

In Mark 7:34, we find Jesus in the midst of working a healing. The text affirms that Jesus gave a deep sigh, and again in 8:12 he sighed deeply. The word translated "sigh" here is the same word as "groan" in Romans 8:22-23 and 26. The word was a technical term in the Hellenistic world of the day for prayer that did not involve the mind but was called forth by the Spirit.

In verse 26, the Spirit is giving vicarious intercession for the saints. Remember, "praying in the Spirit" is presupposed elsewhere in the New Testament (1 Corinthians 14:13; Ephesians 6:18; Jude 20). This "praying in the Spirit" is the same as "praying in tongues." The gift of tongues in 1 Corinthians 14:7-12 and 22, which had a place in public worship, is here described in terms of groans which words cannot express. In short, they are utterances in tongues.

It is the Spirit Himself who is acting here. The utterances in tongues are the medium through which He cries on our behalf to God. The Spirit does not free us from earthly things, but as our proxy brings our needs to God in ways which we cannot express ourselves. While First Corinthians leaves one with a somewhat distasteful attitude towards tongues, Romans affirms tongues with certainty and a positive interpretation. Just as those who spoke in tongues at Corinth required an interpreter to make their utterances intelligible to men (1 Corinthians 14:13, 26), so in Romans those who sigh in prayer need the Spirit as an intercessor in order to make their utterances intelligible to God.

There is one thing here to keep in mind: the Spirit helps us in our "weakness." This kind of prayer is not a sign that the Church has arrived at some kind of spiritual advancement; it is rather a place to begin—a starting place, not a place to end. The honest truth is that for most of the Church today the place to begin has been a source of contention rather than a fount of conciliation.

HANNAH'S CRY

Hannah's prayer in 1 Samuel 1:12 and following sounds much like prayer in the Spirit. The text declares, "As she kept on praying to the Lord, Eli observed her mouth. Hannah was praying in her heart and her lips were moving but her voice was not heard. Eli thought she was drunk with wine." "I am a woman who is deeply troubled. I have not been drinking wine or beer; I was pouring out my soul to the Lord."

In the New Testament, what is recorded in Romans is no different than what Paul calls, "praying in the Spirit." Praying in the Spirit is one of those gracelets that Jesus gives to His children to express the inexpressible in a language given by the Sprit. A subject, which is not often spoken about, is whether Jesus prayed in the Spirit, and certainly it is a debatable point and usually heated.

But as we look here at the story of Hannah, pouring her heart out to the Lord in a desperate situation, she cries out for the Father to hear her. We often can look and make assumptions as Eli thought Hannah was drunk when in fact she was pouring her heart out to the Lord.

The utterances in tongues are the medium through which He (the Spirit) cries on our behalf to God. The Spirit does not free us from earthly things, but as our proxy brings our needs to God in ways which we cannot express ourselves.

ALL THE HELP WE CAN GET

In 1 Corinthians 14:27, we find the "he" of this verse as surely being God the Father. As we begin to "groan" as the Spirit is praying through us, the Father to whom the prayer is addressed immediately reads the mind of the Spirit, for it is his own mind. The Spirit prays in accordance with God's will. He prays this way because we do not know what the will

81

of God is for us.

William Barclay (1955, The Letter to the Romans) says that there are two reasons why we do not know what to pray. First, we cannot pray correctly because we cannot see the future. This often leads to our praying for things that the Father knows are not good for us, things that can bring harm to us. Second, we cannot pray correctly because in any given situation we do not know what is best for us. We do not know our own true needs because we cannot grasp the infinite plan of God for our lives.

We need all the help we can get, and God has graciously provided that help for us by giving us the Holy Spirit to intercede for us while we remain in the present evil age.

THE CHURCH'S MINISTRY OF INTERCESSORY PRAYER

The corporate prayer of the Church in Acts 4 demonstrates a model for intercessory prayer. When the Jews had released Peter and John, they returned and reported to the Church what had happened to them. Luke records that they "raised their voices together in prayer to God." Luke uses the word "raised" in the same way on another occasion in Luke 17:13, where he tells us that the ten lepers called out in a loud voice. The word could actually be translated in this text as "shouted." There is no reason not to understand the word here as meaning praying aloud. It may be offensive for some of us to think in terms of all praying together out loud; however, it seems apparent that this was in fact what took place in Acts 4 as they gathered together.

The second thing we see here in this passage is that while praying out loud, they were all praying the same issue. It was not a time of everyone praying about whatever was closest to his heart, or even about his own needs. It was a time when they together interceded for the issue at hand (e.g. speaking the name of Jesus).

Another point to be made here is that Luke may be recording the sense of the prayer in larger and broader categories, while at the same time capturing some of the very words spoken.

THE HOLY SPIRIT IN PRAYER

Let's look at the text in Acts 4 and how the disciples prayed. First, they reminded God of who He is (v.24); second, they reminded God of what He had done (v.24); third, they reminded God of what He had said (v.25b-26); fourth, they reminded God of the things that had happened to Jesus while He was on the earth (vv.27-28); fifth, they reminded God of the threats they had received (v.29a); sixth, they made their request (v.29b-30); and seventh, there was an answer to their intercessory request (v.31).

It is interesting to me that the Church today rarely prays in this manner. I've been in hundreds of prayer meetings and have heard all kinds of prayers from prayers for traveling mercies to unspoken requests. Those things that characterize prayer in the Church today are rarely seen in the New Testament. A glaring example is prayer for the unsaved. In the New Testament, there is hardly a text that deals with prayer for the lost. Almost all the prayer deals with the needs of the Church itself, for boldness, holiness, power, etc.

The first part of Acts 4 informs us that Peter and John were preaching that Jesus had been raised from the dead. This caused fervor among the leaders and led to their arrest, imprisonment and trial. Luke records that Peter addressed them as "Rulers" in verse 8, and Paul uses this same word in 1 Corinthians 2:6-8 to speak of the "rulers of this age." The common census of commentators is that Paul had in mind the demonic powers behind the "rulers" in this passage. There are at least two things which make me conclude that Luke may have had the same meaning behind the use of the word here in Acts 4:8. First, Luke and Paul were co-workers and certainly knew each other's thoughts concerning matters. And second, Acts was written after 1 Corinthians, and Paul could certainly have influenced Luke. If this is the case, then here in Acts 4:23-31 we have a certified case of the Church entering into intercessory prayer because they were in the midst of spiritual warfare.

So what does all this teach us? We have learned that intercession is always going on! Jesus is praying, and the Holy Spirit is praying! Jesus is praying on our behalf, and the Holy Spirit needs each of us as His instrument. Our responsibility is to allow the Holy Spirit to use us at His determination to intercede for ourselves as well as for others.

How can we intercede? Follow the model of Acts 4:23-31. First, learn to pray aloud and together as a church. Second, address ourselves to God and help our ability to believe by: reminding God of who He is, reminding God of what He has done, reminding God of what His Word says, reminding God of events in the life of Jesus, reminding God of the circumstances we are in and then asking God for the need at hand. It's also important to expect God to act on our behalf of our request.

THE MODEL PRAYER LIFE OF JESUS

When one considers prayer, the model of Jesus must be considered. Jesus is the premier example for the person desiring to learn to pray. There are twenty-one recorded instances in the four Gospels of Jesus praying and twenty-one passages that report His teaching on the subject of prayer. Certainly, some of these overlap, but it seems to warrant the conclusion that it was important to both Jesus and the Gospel writers.

The Gospel of Luke highlights the prayer life of Jesus. It is true that Luke never states that Jesus prayed in order to show His followers how they should pray, but he has also given a number of hints, which make this conclusion all but inevitable.

Luke records ten times that Jesus prayed. In seven of these passages, the prayers are not recorded. Luke also shares two parables, which are unique to him concerning the teaching on prayer (Luke 11:5-8; 18:1-8). All of the references to prayer in Luke are associated with important events in the life of Jesus.

JESUS' TIME WITH THE FATHER

In Luke 3:21-22, we find Jesus praying at His baptism. The text says that while He was praying, the Holy Spirit came. The actual prayer of Jesus is not recorded, but it may be useful to ask the question whether the words of the Father in verse 22 were not in some way a response to whatever Jesus was praying.

And then in Luke 5:15-16 it reads, "He withdrew to the wilderness to pray." Again the text does not specify what He prayed but tells us where, and possibly why, He prayed. While Mark suggests that Jesus went away to avoid the crowds, Luke has correctly seen the positive point. The purpose in seeking seclusion was in order to pray. There is apparently no special reason for the prayer, but in light of Luke 4:42, it may be said that Jesus was unwilling to yield to the temptation to stay in any given place after he had preached to the people lest He might become their popular idol.

Remember, the mainspring of His life was His communion with the Father. In such communion, He must have found both strength and guidance to avoid submitting to temptation. We can learn from this several things: 1) Praying after an event may be just as important as praying before. It might be more important. 2) Seclusion in order to give full attention to the task at hand is surely helpful. 3) Praying after ministering will refocus our attention on the source of the ministry that we have been involved in and not on what we may have done. 4) Prayer is also our wellspring to continued life in God.

GUIDANCE FROM THE FATHER

Luke 6:12 records, "One of those days Jesus went out to a mountainside to pray and spent the night praying to God." Luke has not reported any time periods until now where he says that Jesus prayed all night before He made his momentous decision the next morning when He called all His disciples to Him and chose the twelve that were designated to become apostles. Again Luke does not record the substance of the prayer, but it seems likely that it must surely have included a petition for guidance from God.

We then see in Luke 9:18-22 Luke showing us that Jesus was praying, and His disciples were with Him. Jesus again models prayer before His disciples; however, the prayer is not recorded. It seems apparent that Jesus is asking for divine guidance before making the decisive revelation that follows. He must ask God how He is to go about the task, and if it is the right occasion.

PRAYER AND THE SUPERNATURAL

Luke 9:28-29 reads, "About eight days after Jesus said this, He took Peter, John, and James with him and went up onto a mountain to pray. As He was praying, the appearance of His face changed, and His clothes became as bright as a flash of lightning."

Here we see Jesus taking three of His closest friends to a place of solitude to pray. While He is praying, a divine revelation of Himself to His friends occurs. Again the content of the prayer is not given, but the result sure is. While in prayer, Jesus is caught up into the presence of God. His disciples see Him as they have never seen Him before! It must have blown their doors off! What they saw in Jesus' transfiguration was the very presence of the glory of God being reflected as Jesus was praying. Prayer and supernatural events—they often go together!

In Luke 10:17-21 when the seventy-two returned from their mission and gave Jesus their report, Luke tells us that Jesus was inspired with joy by the Spirit (v.21). The force of the text is that Jesus was filled with joy and with the Spirit before He prayed. What follows is a thanksgiving psalm in which Jesus praised God for something He had done. There seems to be a note of spontaneity in this prayer of Jesus. He was giving God praise for making the words and works of the Kingdom obscure in their significance to one group, while they had been revealed to another group—His disciples. Can't you just hear the excitement in the voice of Jesus? "I praise you, Father, Lord of heaven and earth, because you have hidden these things from the wise and the learned, and revealed them to little children. Yes, Father for this was your good pleasure."

MODELING WHAT IS TAUGHT

Luke 11:1-2 says, "One day Jesus was praying in a certain place. When He finished one of His disciples said to Him, 'Lord, teach us to pray, just as John taught his disciples.' He said to them, 'When you pray say: Father, hallowed be thy name, your kingdom come, give us each day our daily bread. Forgive us our sins, for we also forgive everyone who sins against us. And lead us not into temptation.'"

The words of Jesus' prayer are not recorded here for us, but the text tells us that after they saw Jesus pray—remember this was not the first time—they asked Him to teach them how to pray. Why would His disciples ask him to teach them to pray if they had not seen the results from the prayers of Jesus? The prayer which is often called "The Lord's Prayer" is a model for prayer. Trying to teach others how to pray without letting them see you pray yourself will not work effectively. Remember, the model that Jesus used for teaching was show and tell.

If we want others to learn, then we must also model to them what we want to teach. Jesus not only did this with prayer; He did this with all ministry. He taught the disciples and then often demonstrated what He was teaching.

PRAYER FOR PETER

Luke 22: 31-32 reads, "Simon, Simon, Satan has asked to sift you as wheat. But I have prayed for you Simon that your faith may not fail. And when you have turned back, strengthen your brothers."

Here in the text, Luke informs us at the beginning of Chapter 22 that Satan entered Judas, a believer and one of the Twelve.

The point of the sifting was to find an access point, and Jesus prayed that Peter's fall would not be fatal.

Then he shares the story of the Last Supper. In verse 21, Jesus tells Peter that Satan has asked to sift all of the disciples. The word "you" is plural. The word "asked" means "to demand the surrender of." The background of the thought is surely Job 1:6ff. The idea of sifting was to determine the good wheat from the bad weeds, and Satan wanted to sift Peter and the disciples in order to discover their weakest point, their point of surrender.

The point of the sifting was to find an access point, and Jesus prayed that Peter's fall would not be fatal. This is a true picture of a pastor's heart. He knows his people and knows what their problems are. This enables Him to pray with some direction concerning the flock, which

God has given Him to shepherd.

PRAYER IN SUFFERING

Luke 22: 39-46 reads, "Jesus went out as usual to the Mount of Olives and His disciples followed Him. On reaching the place, He said to them, 'Pray that you will not fall into temptation.' He withdrew about a stone's throw beyond them, knelt down and prayed, 'Father, if you are willing, take this cup from me; yet not my will but yours be done.' An angel from heaven appeared to Him and strengthened Him. And being in anguish, He prayed more earnestly, and His sweat was like drops of blood falling to the ground. When He rose from prayer and went back to the disciples, He found them asleep, exhausted from sorrow. 'Why are you sleeping?' He asked them. 'Get up and pray so that you will not fall into temptation.'"

We are all familiar with this prayer. We should note that Jesus gave His disciples some instructions on how they should pray in this present circumstance. Here we come face-to-face with a man in agony realizing that death was close at hand. In this, we see the humanity of Jesus in prayer, as He struggled to find some other way to accomplish the will of God. He is faced with a human desire to avoid the path of suffering appointed by God. Nevertheless, He accepts the will of God despite His own desire that might be otherwise.

When His will and God's will are aligned in the midst of the struggle, the Father sends an angel to minister to Him and strengthen Him. The effect of the angelic visit is not that Jesus is relieved from the battle of prayer, but that He is able to pray more earnestly. The enemy's attack is overcome by more prayer, and when the intensity of the battle is at its most heated point, the battle will be won or lost in prayer. This was the most powerful spiritual battle in all of history. What was won here in prayer in the spirit world would soon be acted out in the physical world!

Luke gives us insight into the intensity of the battle by telling us that the agony of Jesus found physical expression in sweat that appears like drops of blood falling on the ground. The language here would indicate that this is a metaphorical expression; Jesus was not bleeding as He was praying, as this would undermine His crucifixion. His blood was yet to be spilt in beatings upon the cross itself.

PRAYING ON THE CROSS

Luke 23:34, 46 reads, "Jesus said, 'Father, forgive them, for they do not know what they are doing'," and "Jesus called out with a loud voice, 'Father, into your hands I commit my Spirit.' When he had said this, he breathed His last."

Jesus prays two different prayers from the cross. First, He prays for His enemies (v.34), and second, He petitions God to receive Him (v.46). From the beginning of His ministry at baptism to the close of His ministry on the cross, prayer is continually on the lips of Jesus. He was first and foremost a man of prayer, and He has called us into the same kind of reality.

Jesus was always cognizant of the Father, ever aware that His call was to fulfill the Father's will. He instructed us to pray also that the Father's will be done here on earth. Prayer must be constant in our lives, even as it was in the life of our model, Jesus.

A FRIEND AT MIDNIGHT

The parable found in Luke 11:5-8 is often called "the Friend at Midnight." The interpretation turns on the translation of the word *anaideia*. When it is properly understood, the parable makes sense and has a different meaning from that usually seen in popular interpretations. The parable opens with a question expecting an emphatic negative answer. The question can be paraphrased: "Can you imagine having a guest and going to a neighbor to borrow bread, and the neighbor offers several ridiculous excuses about a locked door and sleeping children?" Someone from the Middle East would respond, "No, I cannot imagine such a thing!"

Contemporary exegetical literature is full of references to the need to travel by night because of the heat. This is true in certain desert areas, but it was not customary in Palestine. The arrival of a friend at midnight is unusual. When a friend did arrive unexpectedly, he was not simply a guest of the individual to whose house he had come, but he was a guest to the whole community. In going to his neighbor, the host is asking the sleeper to fulfill his duty to the guest of the village. With this background in mind, verse 7 should become clearer. In verse 5-7 we have the question, which expects the negative answer. Jesus is saying, "Can you imagine having a friend and going to him with the request to help you entertain a guest, and then he offers silly excuses about sleeping and a barred door?" "No!" would be the reply.

As already stated, the significance of the passage turns on the meaning of the word anaideia in verse 8. The word usually means "shamelessness", but it is translated in most Bibles today as "persistence." The negative meaning of the Greek word certainly raises a problem in the interpretation. Is it "shameless" for the believer to take his request to God in prayer? Surely not! To make sense of the parable, the Church apparently felt it necessary to turn this negative word into a positive one, and by the twelfth century the shift had occurred.

What then is the solution? Another translation of the word is possible. It could be translated "avoidance of shame." Most people read the parable and think that the sleeper finally gave in to the persistence of the host who was making the request. This is an unfortunate reading of the text. The qualities in verse 8 are the qualities of the sleeper, not the host. If the sleeper refuses the request of anything so humble as a loaf of bread, the host would continue his rounds, cursing the stinginess of the sleeper who would not get up to fulfill his duty. The story would be all over the village by morning, and the sleeper would be met with cries of "shame" everywhere he went. Keep in mind if he had not given the bread, he would have brought shame on the entire community as well as himself. Therefore, because of his desire for avoidance of shame, he will arise and grant whatever the borrower wants.

So what does this teach us if it does not teach us persistence in prayer? I believe it can teach us two things. First, it teaches us something about the character of God, that He will answer prayer because of His integrity. Everything was weighted against the host getting his request answered: it was night, it was late and his neighbor was in bed. This made the request awkward but not impossible. Therefore, because of the neighbor's integrity and avoidance of shame, he graciously replied. Our cultural presupposition in the last half of the twentieth century tends to make us uneasy about seeing the preservation of honor as a virtue that is appropriate to God. Given the importance of this concept in the Eastern value system, it would be surprising if Jesus did not use such a quality as a prime virtue for the Father.

Second, this parable teaches us that we can be assured of an answer. If you are confident that you will have your needs met when you go to a neighbor in the night, how much more should you trust God to supply an answer to your needs? God has committed Himself to us as family and has obligated Himself to meet our needs. The parable then teaches us that God is a God of honor and that man can have complete assurance that his prayers will be heard.

THE PERSISTENT WIDOW

The meaning of this parable is succinctly given in verse 1: "Then Jesus told His disciples a parable to show them that they should always pray and not give up." This parable has two characters. The judge was corrupt as indicated by the statement that he did not fear God or regard man. The point was that he did not take the judgment of God seriously. The second character is a widow, a needy and helpless person.

This lady came repeatedly to the judge with a request that he would take up her case. The widow did not want the punishment of the offender but payment of whatever was due to her. For a long time her pleas were in vain, and the judge was legally required to give precedence to her as a widow. He was either unwilling to do so, or did not dare because of the power of her opponent. Finally, he gave in because he feared that she would keep on coming. The parable itself has no application, but we are provided one by Jesus in the following verses (6-8). The parable is concerned with two points: 1) Will God vindicate His people? The answer of course is "Yes!" He will do so because it is His character to do so, not like the judge who was forced to act contrary to his character. 2) Will God's people have to wait long? The answer is that God is not like the judge who had to be pestered before he gave in to the widow. He will answer soon. "Quickly" should be translated "soon," which means that something occurs in a very short period of time. To those waiting it may seem long, but from God's perspective it is not so.

There is an abrupt shift, which occurs in verse 8b. A question is asked, but no answer is given. The question: "When Jesus returns, will there continue to be the faithfulness which is expressed in unfailing prayer?" I believe that this was a real concern for Jesus. When I look at the Church today, it makes sense to me that He would ask this question. Will there be faith on Earth when the Son of Man returns? Will there be prayer that is characterized by faith? Will you and I take seriously the application of this teaching and begin effectively learning to pray, calling out to God night and day, giving Him no rest?

DO WHAT JESUS DID

Solitude. It is striking just how very public the public life of Jesus was. Continually, the Gospels report, Jesus is followed by crowds, surrounded by crowds and literally hounded by them. The reason is understandable: where Jesus was, there was the presence and the power of God. People's lives were being changed. Some received acceptance like the woman at the well (John 4:1-26) and the woman caught in adultery (John 7:53- 8:11). Some received physical healing, as did the leper in (Mark 1:40-45), and some received deliverance like the Capernaum demoniac (Mark 1:21-28).

The pressure on Jesus must have been enormous. Public people have little time for themselves. No wonder Jesus insisted on times alone when He could communicate with the Father.

The times of solitude which Jesus took were not just intermittent escapes because the pressure had become too intense to continue. They were a regular, habitual part of the life of Jesus.

Private Preparation for Power. Oftentimes we think of prayer only as the avenue of getting something for which we feel we have need. The model of Jesus seems to imply that prayer was an avenue through which He could receive reinforcements after a time of ministry in order to take the next step of ministry. Jesus seemed to know that if He was going to minister in power on a continual basis, He needed to meet God on a continual basis.

In Mark's passage (1:35), he shows Jesus as ministering in power: He expels the demon from the man in the synagogue, He heals Peter's mother-in-law and He heals many people at the close of the Sabbath. Early the next morning, we find Jesus seeking a quiet place of prayer. The solitary place where Jesus prayed is interesting. The place where he went to pray was certainly a physical place, but the words with which Mark chooses to describe it do not mean a geographic place. The word carries profound theological insights. The description resembles the description of the place of Jesus' temptation. In His temptation, as well as here, He was preparing for further ministry, and Mark shares that with his readers.

Mark mentions Jesus praying only three times in his gospel: in chapter one, after the feeding of the five thousand, in chapter six and in Gethsemane in chapter fourteen. It appears that Mark's account is to show the source of Jesus' power against illness and demons and also to provide in Jesus' behavior an example to his readers of earnest and dedicated times of private preparation with God.

If we are to do the works of Jesus, we must do all of them. One of His works, which is difficult for us to come to grips with, is his private preparation in order to continue the ministry of power. Martin Luther spent an hour at the beginning of each day in prayer, but if he anticipated an unusually hard day, he prayed longer. So often we let a busy schedule interfere with our times of communication with God. We need to look at our schedules and find out if a bit more discipline might help.

Private Preparation Takes Discipline. Discipline: such an appetizing subject! The word has become a dirty word in our culture. It often suggests regimentation under compulsion, a mindless following of the program—it is necessary for kids, not for adults!

The tyranny of the urgent stands in our way! This reminds me of the story about the farmer who went out to gather his eggs for the day. While he was walking toward the hen house, he noticed that his water pump was leaking. He stopped to fix it, only to find out that it needed a new washer. Off to the barn he went to fetch one. While moving in that direction, he noticed that the hayloft needed some straightening, so he went to find his pitchfork. Hanging next to the pitchfork was a broom, which had a broken handle. He thought it might be good to write himself a note, so he went back to his house to jot one down. As he opened the door, the hinge squeaked loudly, and he began to look in the kitchen for some oil when his wife requested that he go and get some eggs for breakfast. Sound familiar?

Hebrews 12:11 tells us, "No discipline seems pleasant at the time, but painful. Later on, however, it produces a harvest of righteousness and peace for those who have been trained by it." Discipline does hurt, but it brings the gain we need in our lives. We need a disciplined prayer life. By that I don't mean a rigid or mechanical one; we must see the pattern of Jesus in the initiation of God for our own lives.

The times of private preparation brought power for ministry into His life. He found time, so can we!

Seven

FAMILY TALK

"BLOOM WHERE YOU'RE PLANTED"

Marriage should be honored by all, and the marriage bed kept pure, for God will judge the adulterer and all the sexually immoral" (Hebrews 13:4). If first-century Jews steeped in the laws of Moses and pressured by a conservative religious community needed to hear this advice, how much more do we need to take it to heart?

Our current American culture is hostile to faithful monogamous marriage. On one hand, we may embrace the secularized philosophy of personal growth and self-fulfillment regardless of the cost to our marriage and family. On the other hand, the most committed and well-meaning of us are barraged daily with sensual images in ads, television and movies. There is an ever-present pressure to be unfaithful in search of new excitement. Yet we are reminded that adultery and fornication are not only social sins against one's marriage partner, they are moral and spiritual sins that deserve the very judgment of God.

In honoring marriage, God would have us guard not only our outward behavior but also our minds and hearts. There is no place for the pattern of lust outside or inside marriage. It is sad but true that in many cases the lovemaking of the Church has been corrupted by the world, resulting in wounded relationships and abuse.

God has provided the physical relationship in marriage not only for procreation and enjoyment but also that we might minister to one another. We need to look to the Lord to purify and cleanse the physical relationship in marriage. Remember that marriage is to mirror the sacred relationship between God and the Church. With God's help we can approach our marriage with the same selfless commitment, respect and tenderness we see in His love for us as His bride, the Church.

How do we overcome these challenges of keeping our Christian principles in Western society today? Jesus taught that God wanted strong marriages that lasted a lifetime. In Matthew 19:3-9, the Pharisees asked Him if it was lawful for a man to divorce his wife for any reason. He responded:

"Haven't you read...that at the beginning the Creator 'made them male and female,' and said, 'for this reason a man will leave his father and mother and be united to his wife, and the two shall become one flesh?' So they are no longer two, but one. Therefore what God has joined together, let no man separate" (Matthew 19:4-6).

Marriage is something that God created. Men and women who walk away from it violate God's will. Jesus rooted His answer in the Word of God, referring back to the creation accounts in Genesis 1:27 and 2:24. In Scripture we too discover and understand God's purpose and plan for marriage. What does the Word of God teach us about building strong families?

CHRISTIAN VALUES

One of the foremost challenges to family life in Western society is the loss of Christian principles and values. Our culture no longer promotes a Christian way of life, and in many ways it deliberately attempts to undermine Christian values.

A willingness to serve and submit to one another is the hallmark of successful Christian families.

Turn on the TV, go to the movies or pick up magazines to see how adultery, homosexuality, fornication and divorce are all presented as okay. Money is proclaimed as the key to happiness. Get as much power as you can. Live for today. Live for yourself.

The pace of life also leads to family fragmentation. Jobs, school and extra-curricular activities leave little time for family life. Fathers and mothers limit family involvement due to the demands of their jobs.

Parents are discouraged about how to raise children. They are confused over what to do about discipline, friends, school, the media, clothes, drugs and sex. Many of them give up, viewing their children's teen years as a lost battle.

There is no clearer passage of Scripture about family life than Ephesians 5:21-6:4. It begins, "Submit to one another out of reverence to Christ." Jesus' life was characterized by servant hood. He emptied himself and took on the nature of a servant in order to "give his life as a ransom for many" (Matthew 20:28). A willingness to serve and submit to one another is the hallmark of successful Christian families (see Philippians 2:2-4).

Let's take a look at those instructions in Ephesians 5:22-6:4 in which Paul offers specific instructions for wives, husbands, parents and children.

Wives. Ephesians 5:22-24 says, "Wives submit to your husbands as to the Lord. For the husband is the head of the wife as Christ is the head of the church, his body, of which he is the Savior. Now as the church submits to Christ, so also wives should submit to their husbands in everything."

Until the rise of the modern feminist movement in the 1960's, Christians did not consider this a controversial or difficult passage to understand. Paul taught that the wife is to be submitted to her husband and respect him because she is one with him (see Ephesians 5:31), and the Church's attitude toward Christ is a model for how she should submit to and respect her husband.

Before discussing what submission means, it is important to know what it doesn't mean. First, it doesn't mean the wife is of lesser value than her husband. Western culture tends to equate function with personal worth. But we need to look only as far as God Himself to see that submission does not mean inferiority of worth. Jesus said, "The world must know that I love the Father and that I do exactly what my Father has commanded me" (John 14:31).

Jesus was submitted to His Father in all things, and yet He was fully God: "I and the Father are one" (John 10:30). Jesus submitted to His Father for the sake of unity and because He loved Him. In no way did His submission make Him any less than fully God.

In 1 Corinthians 11:3, Paul draws a parallel between the family of the Trinity and the human family: "Now I want you to realize that the head of every man is Christ, and the head of every woman is man, and the head of Christ is God." Just as Jesus remains fully God in a submitted relationship to the Father, so wives are not any less human as they submit in love to their husbands.

Second, the submission of a wife to her husband is not the same as submission of women as a class to men. Third, Scripture nowhere teaches that wives are to submit to unscriptural demands from their husbands. They are to reject unnatural and abusive sexual demands and other forms of verbal and physical mistreatment. In instances where husbands have fallen into drug or alcohol abuse, wives may for a while, if not permanently, have to separate from them. Furthermore, wives have a responsibility to protect their children from abusive fathers.

Submission does mean a wife is a willing, loving and respectful giver of her heart to her husband. Peter even says that, wherever possible, this should also be true for Christian wives of non-Christian husbands (1 Peter 3:1-7). In fact, he teaches that Christian wives can win their non-Christian husbands to the Lord through loving, respectful and submissive behavior.

Proverbs 31 is perhaps the best description of a wife found in the Bible. She is described as "a wife of noble character" who is a successful and aggressive businesswoman (Proverbs 31:10). She works hard, reaches out to the poor, supports her husband, speaks with wisdom and teaches, oversees her household and is respected by her children. She is a full partner with her husband in advancing the Kingdom of God.

Husbands. Next, Paul turns his attention to the responsibility of the husbands: "Husbands, love your wives, just as Christ loved the church and gave himself up for her to make her holy, cleansing her by the washing with water through the word, and to present her to himself as a radiant church, without stain or wrinkle or any other blemish, but holy and blameless. In this same way, husbands ought to love their wives as their own bodies. He who loves his wife loves himself...however, each one of you also must love his wife as he loves himself, and the wife must respect her husband" (Ephesians 5:25-28, 33).

While husbands are exhorted to love their wives, there isn't a single verse in Scripture that commands wives to love their husbands. (Though Titus 2:4 does say that older women should train younger women to love their husbands.) There's a reason for this. When husbands truly love and honor their wives, wives usually respond by loving their husbands.

I believe that the primary reason for the disintegration of family life in

Western culture today can be traced to the failure of husbands to love their wives with sacrificial love. But how do we do this? Paul says, Look at the love Christ has for the Church.

As we have already seen, Jesus was submitted to His heavenly Father in all things. For husbands to be the leaders of their families, they must first be submitted to Jesus Christ in all things. Submitted men actively cultivate the spiritual disciplines of prayer, Scripture study and meditation, and fasting in their lives. They are full of faith, hope and courage, eager to obey God's Word. They are gracious and willingly submit to spiritual leaders.

> When husbands truly love and honor their wives, wives usually respond by loving their husbands.

There are other qualities about Jesus' love for the Church that reveal how husbands should love their wives.

- Christ died for the Church to save it. A husband should be willing to die to his personal needs and desires for the good of the wife.

- Christ makes the Church holy. A husband should be willing to do whatever he has to for his wife to be a strong woman of God. A man who approaches marriage on the basis of what it can do for himself does not understand the true nature of being a Christian husband.

- Christ loves the Church as Himself. A husband should think of his wife as a part of himself, not merely as someone he happens to be living with and who has a separate life. In practice this means husbands should cultivate an intimate relationship with their wives (see Colossians 3:19; 1 Peter 3:7).

- Christ gives the Church direction and guidance. A Christian husband should be a leader. He should be willing to take on responsibility for his wife and their life together, which includes their children. This means setting direction and making decisions.

LOVING YOUR HUSBAND (by Carol Wimber)

Titus 2:3-5 says, "Likewise, teach the older women to be reverent in the way they live, not to be slanders or addicted to too much wine, but to teach what is good. Then they can train the younger women to love their husbands and children, to be self-controlled and pure, to be home-makers, to be kind, and to be subject to their husbands, so that no one will malign the Word of God."

Genesis 1:27 tells us that back in the beginning God created male and female, and it was very good. In chapter two God says that "it's not good for man to be alone, so he made a suitable helper for him." Now, be careful here not to hear the word "servant." The same word is used in other passages such as in Hebrews 13:6: "The Lord is my helper, and I will not be afraid."

The word used here is *ezer*, and it is used two times for woman and over a dozen times of God Himself.

The Curse. First, it's important that we look at the curse. Genesis 2:20b-3:18 gives us a breakdown:

- Genesis 3:12: Observe the influence woman has.

- Genesis 3:16: "desire for her husband" — her desire (dependency, emotional security, identity, well-being) had been centered in the Lord Himself, but now, because of separation from God, the husband becomes the object of all these things, in effect her "god."

- Genesis 3:17: man now transfers his focus from relationship with God and was now focused on what he could achieve in life (identity, security, coming from his achievements, his work). The relationship he had with God was cut off, and his achievements became a god to him. No wonder so many men commit suicide when their business fails!

Let Him Off the Hook. God's intention was to have two separate and different creatures, both getting their identity and security as well as their needs met by God due to their relationship with Him. For those of us who are born again, that curse is broken, and we have the choice to let God be God, not our husbands. In fact, let him off the hook! It's lonely being a god, and he needs your friendship and help. God has given you this man, not another, to love. He has entrusted to you this man.

Love the husband you have, and forget the one you thought you had; he's a figment of your imagination. You need to get your emotional dependency off the poor guy and get it on Jesus! Forget the, "I married the wrong man" idea. The man you are married to now is the right man! This is the marriage that Jesus wants to redeem. And the good news is that it doesn't depend on the response of the husband. He can be a rotten husband, but you can still be a good wife by loving him! Remember what Jesus said? "Whatever you do for the least of these, you do for me" (Matthew 25:40). Remember, it is the Lord Jesus Christ you serve.

Every Christian wife has been given the responsibility from God to love her husband as he is, not needing him to be god for her. We're not to place ourselves in the position of being critical or blaming, but instead serving our husbands in love. If you won't serve him, whom will you serve? Because you are commanded by the Lord to submit to your husband, you live in the dignity of your relationship to God when you do submit willingly.

Everyone submits to someone. That is the order of God. Whether it be children to parents, wife to husband, citizens to government, Jesus to the Father or all of us to God. Hebrews 5:7-8 says, "Jesus called out with loud cries and tears to the one who could save him from death, and He was heard because of his reverent submission." What we do in our marriages has more to do with our love for Jesus than our love for our husbands.

The Importance of Healthy Sexual Relations. Enough books have been written in the last several years to fill a library about the discovery that women can and even do enjoy sex. With patient love and the interest of her husband, a woman can reach the full sexual enjoyment that God intended for her.

Okay, so what about the woman whose husband has been patient, loving and understanding and still the woman has trouble responding sexually to him?

I want to tell you something about your husband. If you haven't been loving him in an active, participating way sexually, he isn't a very happy man. I don't care how much his pride would make him deny it, that man feels lousy on the inside where he keeps all his male self-worth.

Ladies, your husband is made so that sex is very, very important to him. He needs to know that he is a marvelous lover and that he excites you and satisfies you.

Now, unless he's been living in a jungle for the last ten years or so, he has probably read some of the "how to" manuals on sex, and when that didn't make him any more exciting to you, he came to the conclusion that he really is an inferior man, a mediocre lover, or worse! No sense in asking him all about it because rarely would a man admit those kind of fears.

We ladies generally think of our husbands as the "reasonable" one and ourselves as the "emotional" half in our marriage, but truthfully, a man does not decide what kind of a man he is in his "reason center" or "intellect"; he knows what kind of a man he is by the way you respond to him. Actually this of course goes for every area of marriage, but don't underestimate the sexual aspect of your relationship with him. It's a BIG deal to him! You can be a great wife in every other way (as this often is the pattern). You might be a fine cook, a good housekeeper, an excellent mother, proud of his ability as a provider and yet do him in by not responding to him in bed. And it does do him in although most men, rather than admit their worst fear that they don't "cut it" as a man, will retreat emotionally and cover up their pain. Men are still little boys inside.

That's an old trite saying, but it's an old trite feeling too when an emotional slap-in-the-face is handed out. Your husband needs to be told, and actions speak louder than words, how great he is. Even if he is five foot two and weighs 118 pounds, he needs to know he is "great" in your eyes, and he judges how "great" he is by your response to his lovemaking. If your husband hasn't any apparent interest in making love, then someone or some circumstance has killed that very basic male need in him.

More than likely it has been years of circumstances—usually being turned away by his wife—and years of attitudes that have smothered that male drive in him. Even so, there isn't a man still breathing that can't be brought back to life and made to know what a wonderful man he is. In fact, it's knowing that that brings a man back to life.

All right, now we know how important it is to a man to know that his wife enjoys him sexually. But then how do you get started?

What if, even understanding all this, you still don't have any feeling except guilt when he touches you? You hate the bedroom because it represents "failure" to you. You want to respond, but emotionally you're dead. You hate to put that poor guy through the grueling process again of trying to turn you on.

Every woman, to one degree or another, has had or will have, without God's intervention, this problem. Many women have convinced themselves that they are frigid, although they wonder why it didn't show up until so late? She was great when they were going together, but now that they are married, the thought scares her into thinking that perhaps she really doesn't love her husband. However, many women suffer from this complaint and, let me assure you, it has nothing to do with whether or not they love their husband because otherwise they wouldn't care if they hurt him or not.

So here you are, wanting to love your husband sexually but not really feeling anything. It's strange, but women feel the sexiest right up to the bedroom door; then something happens, and the bedroom becomes a morgue.

Here is your problem: you are waiting to feel. You want to feel, and you think you can't do anything until you feel like it. Do you see it? You are being trapped into thinking that you can't love until your feelings are involved. But the good news is if you act on the basis of your will and forget about your feelings, the feelings or emotions will follow. Do you understand that? Act first, feel later.

And the result is that your husband will go out of his mind with glee! Which in turn makes you feel good. He knows you love him, and he knows he is a man. He'll take on the world. He'll even fix the cupboard door! He is a happy man!

This is such a simple process, but because it is so simple, sometimes we miss the point. Let me go over it again. As mature Christian people, we should always act on a decision of our will. We don't ask ourselves if we "feel" like it before we commit ourselves to certain courses of action. Or, if we do, our lives get pretty sloppy. For example, you haven't been married too long before you find yourself bored with the whole concept of housework, but if you wait to feel differently—like excited about the dirty dishes—well, you can see where that kind of thing will get you. It's really not much use reading, How to do your dishes 420 ways. That might spur you on to a spasmodic effort at first, but the excitement will wear off. Really, the only way to get those dishes done is for you to decide to do them by an act of your will, and then of course, do them.

A strange and lovely thing often follows: you feel so good about your dishes and the nice thing you did for them that maybe you can't wait to do them again! It seems that the more you do your dishes, the more you enjoy it. What's also important about this is the way you feel about yourself. You are pleased with yourself and what you did.

You do things because they need to be done. Good emotions or bad emotions, you do them. Well, your man needs to be loved, and he needs to know you love him. So love him because it needs to be done. Don't wait until you feel like it, just go ahead and start choosing to love him. A marvelous thing will happen as you realize you are free from your emotions. They don't rule you anymore. You can do what you choose, and your feelings will get in line after your will and actions, and you will be flooded by all the right feelings! Do you see where this is also an act of faith?

Now, I know what some of you might be saying to yourselves right now, "You mean, go ahead and begin making love when I don't even feel anything at all?" Yes, that is exactly what I mean, and this time you initiate it. A good place to start making love to your husband is to do what gives him the most pleasure. Remember, ignore your emotions. The reason I say to start with the act that gives him the most pleasure is that this means total commitment, and he feels your commitment, and to him it is translated, "true love."

In suggesting all of this, I am taking for granted that you know God designed your body to give pleasure to your husband. There is nothing wrong with whatever you do together to give one another pleasure or to show your deep commitment and love. God says the marriage bed is sacred. Period.

The lovemaking between you and your husband is a wonderful secret that you share with only God Himself. And God will bless any way you find to express that love to each other.

We all have an idea in the back of our emotions, even if our intellects tell us otherwise, that there are certain sexual acts that are not very nice. Forget all that! It's a lie of the devil designed to hang you both up. A Christian is the only being alive that is able to fully enjoy all the areas of love that God has given us. In the privacy of your bedroom, anything goes. This is assuming that no one has sadistic or masochistic tendencies. I won't go into all of that; besides, in all the instances that we have counseled couples that are afraid they are doing something "sick" or "perverted," they feel guilty over perfectly natural sex acts.

What I am trying to say to you is to love your husband in every and any way, and let him love you. Let him give you pleasure, too, because that's what makes him happy.

The Church is full of Christian women going around busily doing "God's work" or so they believe. Have you ever stopped to realize that the most spiritual thing you can do is to make love to your husband? Do you know what will happen? Your husband will become very "spiritual." Think about it; isn't that the way it should be?

Until you are totally committed to him in every way, you aren't going to free your emotions to do what you want them to do. By putting aside your "Okay, I'm willing, try to excite me" attitude and instead thinking about how you can best give him pleasure, you have put into process the "wheat dying to itself" principle, and you will begin to reap the wonderful results. So don't worry about your emotions, whether they are good or bad; eventually they will line up according to your will. But your goal must be to love and please your husband. That really is reward enough: knowing that he is happy and knowing you're the reason behind it.

In conclusion I would like to quote Mrs. Billy Graham: "You make him happy... God will make him good."

PARENTING (by John & Carol)

Husbands and wives who love each other as Christ loves the Church have a sure foundation for parenthood. Loving marriages produce "good child soil," an environment of love, security and acceptance in which their children grow. Parents' love for their children is enhanced or diminished by how they love each other. Children want to know that their parents love them. Plus they gain security, confidence and their understanding of God's love from mom and dad.

Of course good parenting goes beyond modeling God's love in our marriages. It also involves specific skills. In Ephesians 6:4 Paul writes, "Fathers, do not exasperate your children; instead, bring them up in the training and instruction of the Lord." Father abuse of their children is an age-old problem. Paul warned fathers against exasperating, or embittering, their children, "or they [the children] will become discouraged" (Colossians 3:21). When I pray for people with serious spiritual, emotional, or physical problems, I frequently uncover childhood abuse from their parents.

In recent years the media has acquainted us with obvious forms of abuse, especially beating and sexual molestation. But I suspect a more widespread problem is the breaking of children's spirits from constant criticism, rebuke, nagging and cruel discipline. By exercising strict control over their children as they get older, parents communicate mistrust for and a lack of confidence in them.

The prescription for abusive authority isn't doing away with authority. It's loving discipline. After warning fathers against exasperating their children, Paul instructed them to "bring them up in the training and instruction of the Lord" (Ephesians 6:4). The Greek words translated here "training" and "instruction" mean education by discipline and admonition.

The prescription for abusive authority isn't doing away with authority. It's loving discipline.

The first term, "training," implies much more than merely imparting knowledge; it's a tough term that incorporates discipline. Of course, the training is in Christian living with the goal in mind that when children are adults, they are equipped to live fully for God. The picture Paul paints of a loving father is similar to that of a caring shepherd. Like a pastor with those in his care, a father's goal too should be to train younger Christians so they can love God fully. Shepherds cannot do this unless they exercise loving authority. A father's failure to exercise loving authority makes it difficult for children to receive discipline from their heavenly Father. The writer of Hebrews says discipline from God is a sign that He loves us (Hebrews 12:6-6, quoted from Proverbs 3:11,12).

The Greek word translated "discipline" in this passage is the same word Paul used in Ephesians 6:4, where he instructed fathers to train their children. If we have received loving discipline from our fathers, it is much easier to receive it from our heavenly father; if out of reaction to childhood abuse we run from God's discipline, we will miss out on "a harvest of righteousness and peace for those who have been trained by it" (Hebrews 12:11).

A striking example of a poor harvest can be seen in the lives of Eli, Samuel and David in the Old Testament. Eli failed to discipline his sons, and his whole house reaped judgment (1 Samuel 3:12-13). Then Eli mentored Samuel, and Samuel also failed to discipline his sons (1 Samuel 8:3). Finally, Samuel was King David's spiritual father, and David likewise failed miserably with his children (1 Kings 1:6; 2 Samuel 13:21).

Our Children. Ephesians 6:1-3 says, "Children obey your parents in the Lord, for this is right. Honor your father and mother, which is the first commandment with a promise, that it may go well with you and that you may enjoy long life on the earth."

Children have a responsibility to obey. Western culture encourages children to disrespect their parents and reject their instruction. Almost all forms of discipline or restriction are considered cruel and "limiting to a child's potential." In Sweden parents can be arrested for spanking their children!

But Scripture is clear: children are to respect, honor and receive from their parents the discipline and instruction of the Lord. The purpose is that the children might grow up to be strong citizens of the Kingdom of God, be blessed and live long lives.

The keys to strengthening family life are found in Scripture. If we were to put into action these simple principles, we could overcome many of the challenges that Christian families have to face today. And we would pass along a heritage to our children that would prepare them for the unique challenges of the twenty-first century.

PRACTICAL THINGS
ON RAISING CHILDREN (by Carol Wimber)

John and I had four children: Chris, Tim, Stephanie and Sean. In retrospect the truth is our children raised us. Many of the "hair-raising" times we thought we couldn't live through did us the most good; they sanded off some of the splinters, so to speak. Some of the issues I'll touch on we did right, and many we learned from doing it wrong, and most I suspect, we haven't learned yet.

First of all, prayer is so important. We must pray for our kids. I have to start with prayer because nothing good can happen anywhere unless we pray. I do it like this: God has given me to my husband to be a help to him, and in the process I am blessed. God has given us these children whom He created, for a purpose and whom He loves beyond understanding to me, to love and to care for and to raise for Him. So my husband and my children belong to God, not me. That's my understanding. Therefore, I have the responsibility to ask God what He wants for them, what His plans are for each of them and pray accordingly. When we quit thinking of them as ours, we can pray with some anointing because we aren't praying selfishly.

I also do this little mind thing to help keep me from taking prayer for granted. I think, "What would I do for an hour appointment (okay, half an hour!) with God Himself?" At these times I don't think of God on His throne and me at His feet; (there are other times for that.) I picture myself going into His office and God instructing His secretary to hold all calls and not to disturb us. Then He takes a seat behind the desk, and I take mine on the other side. I think of these times as intimate business meetings understanding that He is all-powerful, but He has entrusted me with this man (my husband) and these children. I give my report as honestly as I can, including my failures to love and help, telling Him my fears for this family member or that one. I ask Him for grace and help, going over again His plan for each one and letting Him reassure me that things are on target. If somehow I have taken control again of my life or theirs (and I am full of the resulting anxiety), then I repent and give them all back to God again.

After thanking Him for the indescribable privilege of being able to meet with Him like this, He gives me instruction and advice. He reminds me of the things He then promised me, and I come away full of peace. That is how I pray for them. Of course there are other times of just gratitude and worship.

Second, I think it's important that you don't ever humiliate your children when disciplining them. Sometimes, because of our own embarrassment and worry about what people will think of us, we overreact or abruptly discipline our children. Take the time to pull them aside or into another room alone and talk to them at their face level.

Third, it is impossible to be guileless and manipulate at the same time. Another impossible thing is to manipulate and be in God's will. Manipulation is hell's way to achieve something. It is anti-trust in God. Many women have tried to control their families by manipulation, especially religious manipulation. It never produces godliness in the children, and it almost always produces buried rage and rebellion. Don't use "God talk" to make your family do what you want them to do. Be real. If you want them to do something, say so. Don't play games like pouting, tears or depression. It is all manipulation, trying to make something happen using your own methods. Don't spiritualize everything. A sure way to bar your husband coming to know the Lord is by being a super-spiritual religious wife.

When it comes to manipulation, the issue is always control. Who will control your life and the lives around you? You? Or God? All manipulation involves pretense, guile, saying and doing to produce a prescribed response in another person. The word "manipulation" means "to handle and control with your hands." Manipulation is acting a certain way so you will get the response you want. "If I say this, then he will say thus and so..."

In Genesis 25:23, the Lord had already told Rebekah that the older son shall serve the younger. Yet she felt she needed to work that out. She was a controlling, manipulative woman, and she raised a controlling, manipulating son. If we wait for God to work things out, there is always blessing. We bring curses and anger down on our head when we manipulate situations. So be transparent and don't pretend.

Fourth, we are to love the husband and the children we have, not the ones we wish we had or wanted them to be. We didn't make our children; they have been given to us to raise and to love.

Fifth, we should be courteous to our family, and we should talk nicely to them just as we would someone we like!

Sixth, we need to be careful, not naïve. Wake up and smell the coffee. Junior High kids should not be left alone. Don't be over-trusting just because you have a Christian kid. And don't be surprised if your kids don't get saved easier than you did.

Seventh, the husband and wife need to love and respect each other. It makes the kids secure while also ratifying your relationship with Jesus for them. The kids know, along with the rest of the world, that any real relationship with Jesus will enable you to love your mate. Anything else is just talk.

Eighth, I would encourage you to live in today. This means you don't live in yesterday, thinking how great or awful it used to be. We aren't to live in tomorrow, hoping and worrying over the future. Be with them all the way now. Don't hurry and wish the present away.

Ninth, we need to listen to our kids. It is one of the greatest gifts you can give another person. You are truly listening when you're not thinking about anything else while they are talking. I know this is quite a trick when you have more than one child, but you can train them to take turns. At least this way they all get heard some of the time instead of nobody being heard any of the time.

If you want the lines of communication to stay open with your husband and your children, then don't choose the times when they are telling you something about their life to correct or make judgments. It will shut them up like a clam!

The tenth important thing in raising kids is not to mortgage your family in this world of "over-rated pleasures and under-rated treasures." These lyrics to an old song express the heart of it. In our culture it is easy to become overextended in every way, and it costs us our family lives. Don't mortgage your family to "keep up with the Joneses." Spend your best time, energy, interest, leisure on your own children and husband. Don't sell your time with them to an employer so you can get a bigger house for them. They would rather have you.

Here's the scene: the phone glued to your ear, all cheerful or concerned with your friend, all the while ignoring the little guy who has been trying to get your attention for the last hour. The heartbreaking reality is that they will give up eventually. Then we will weep over the lost years when they wanted our attention and now they isolate themselves in their bedrooms, having transferred their needs to their peer group or boyfriend or girlfriend, or something worse. We need to be there when it's "Mom, watch me!" or "Watch this!" "See what I can do?" "See how big I am?" Do any of us ever really grow out of that hunger to be observed by the ones we love, doing great and wonderful things that amaze and astound them and cause praise and admiration to flow from their lips? I don't think so. It camouflages itself over the years, but it's still there, so important and yet as a wife or mom, you are the only one equipped for the job.

Many of us save the best for strangers in whose lives we have almost no influence, and we give our own family, in whom we have such deep influence and effect, our leftovers. Who are we going to invest our lives in? Who is more important than our own husbands and children? So, if we save the best of ourselves for others and ration our attention, interest, care, praise, smiles and laughter to the only ones God gave especially to us to care for, we have truly missed it. And they know it too; you can't fool your children.

Eight

BECOMING A
GOOD CHURCHMAN

"DANCE WITH THE ONE WHO BROUGHT YOU"

The New Testament writers employ many analogies to describe the Body of Christ. I think of the church as an army when I read Paul's words in 2 Timothy 2:3, "Endure hardship with us like a good soldier of Christ Jesus."

Other passages of Scripture compare the Church to a hospital, a place where people receive healing for spiritual, physical, emotional and social hurts. "Is any one of you sick?" James asks, "He should call the elders of the church to pray over him" (James 5:14).

Both soldiers and hospital workers need a place to retreat from the rigors of battle and hard work, where they can be renewed and equipped. I think Peter has this in mind when he compares the Church to a family: "For it is time for judgment to begin with the family of God" (1 Peter 4:17). That is, God intends that the Church be a place of positive, loving and accepting relationships, a place where righteousness reigns and in which people know and are known by others. In a word, we all need a place we can call home, and that is the essence of fellowship.

All too often people search for the perfect church, with perfect people with perfect lives. The problem is we all know that's not a reality. It's a choice decision to say "yes" and commit ourselves to what Christ loves and is coming back for. All families have their squabbles from time to time, and the Church is no different. At the end of the day, with all its imperfections the Church is still the best place to be!

The world knows what this is supposed to look like. Years ago in New York City, I got into a taxi cab with an Iranian taxi driver, who could hardly speak English. I tried to explain to him where I wanted to go, and as he was pulling his car out of the parking place, he almost got hit by a van that on its side had a sign reading "The Pentecostal Church." He got really upset and said, "That guy's drunk." I said, "No, he's a Pentecostal. Drunk in the spirit, maybe, but not with wine." He asked, "Do you know about church?" I said, "Well, I know a little bit about it; what do you know?" It was a long trip from one end of Manhattan to the other, and all the way down he told me one horror story after another that he'd heard about the Church. He knew about the pastor that ran off with the choir master's wife, the couple that had burned the church down and collected the insurance—every horrible thing you could imagine.

We finally get to where we were going, I paid him, and as we're standing there on the landing, I gave him an extra-large tip. He got a suspicious look in his eyes—he'd been around, you know. I said, "Answer me this one question." Now keep in mind, I'm planning on witnessing to him. "If there was a God and He had a church, what would it be like?" He sat there for awhile making up his mind to play or not.

Finally he sighed and said, "Well, if there was a God and He had a church—they would care for the poor, heal the sick, and they wouldn't charge you money to teach you the Book."

I turned around, and it was like an explosion in my chest. "Oh, God." I just cried; I couldn't help it. I thought, "Oh Lord, they know. The world knows what it's supposed to be like, and we as the Church don't get it most of the time!"

When you joined the Kingdom, you expected to be used of God. I've talked to thousands of people, and almost everybody has said, "When I signed up, I knew that caring for the poor was part of it—I just kind of got weaned off of it because no one else was doing it." Folks, I'm not saying, "Do something heroic." I'm not saying, "Take on some high standard, sell everything you have and go." Now, if Jesus tells you that, that's different. But I'm not saying that. I'm just saying, participate.

Give some portion of what you have—time, energy, money, on a regular basis—to this purpose, to redeeming people, to caring for people. Share your heart and life with somebody that's not easy to sit in the same car with. Are you hearing me? That's where you'll really see the Kingdom of God.

LOVE ONE ANOTHER

I think we underestimate the power and importance of loving each other. Consistent love for other Christians is key to a healthy spiritual life because loving fellowship is God's prescribed environment for growth. This kind of love is based on commitment to God Himself. To be committed to God is to be committed to His community, the Church. This is not a commitment to the theory of the Church, but to an actual body of other fallible, imperfect people.

Many of us treat church life like immature adolescents. From other Christians we want thrills, constant exhilaration and to have our needs met. When Christian brothers and sisters fall short of our expectations, when they are boring and imperfect and fail to meet our needs for strokes, we pout, turn away and isolate ourselves from them. Jesus calls us to mature commitment of love for His people—the very people in our fellowship!

I have many fond memories and warm thoughts about the fellowship I was a part of as a baby Christian. It is true that the dear people who nursed me through Christian babyhood were not perfect. But their cardinal virtue was the fact that they consistently loved and accepted me even as an immature and messy baby Christian!

Without their love and care, I might have never made it through this crucial time. Like these kind and patient Christians, we need to learn how to keep people through love. Despite imperfections, sins and irritating habits of other Christians, they belong to Jesus and they need our love as a healthy climate for growth.

We are also told to not forget to entertain strangers, for by doing so some have entertained angels without knowing it. Of course, the reference to angels is from the incident in Abraham's life when he welcomed and entertained three strangers who turned out to be angels bringing a message from God. Being hospitable to those outside our immediate circle of Christian friends demonstrates love in a

> **The attitude and act of welcoming a stranger into our lives as well as our homes may bear eternal fruit as well as being a practical form of ministry.**

pure form. In fact, hospitality demonstrates the very heart of Jesus.

In Luke 14:12, Jesus instructs a Pharisee (and us) to invite people to share our hospitality who cannot pay it back. "But when you give a banquet, invite the poor, the crippled, the lame, the blind, and you will be blessed. Although they cannot repay you, you will be repaid at the resurrection of the righteous." This is not the kind of hospitality that worries about making a favorable impression but a desire to share our comforts and blessing with those who need it.

In this age of the pursuit of self-gratification and self-indulgence, genuine, warm hospitality stands out as a practical example of unselfish giving. The attitude and act of welcoming a stranger into our lives as well as our homes may bear eternal fruit as well as be a practical form of ministry.

REMEMBERING FORGOTTEN PEOPLE

It is characteristic of Jesus to remember the people that the world has forgotten. In fact, this seems to be his specialty! We see him embracing untouchable lepers and cleansing them, ministering to those who were spiritual outcasts such as the Gerasene demoniac and reaching out to redeem Matthew, the social outcast tax collector. Even in the agony of the cross, one thief asks, "Jesus, remember me when you come into your kingdom!" And He said to him, "I tell you the truth, today you will be with me in paradise" (Luke 23:42-43).

Jesus urges his followers in Matthew 25:35-40 to remember the prisoners by visiting them, "I was in prison and you came to visit me..." When they asked Him, "When did we see you sick or in prison and go to visit you?" Jesus replies, "Whatever you did for the least of one of these brothers of mine, you did for me." Those in prison are forgotten by society. Many of them are faced daily with remorse for their mistakes and crimes. They are ripe to be remembered and ministered to in Jesus' name. We can be channels of Jesus' love and redemption to these people.

We are also encouraged to remember and minister to the victims of mistreatment. These occasions may be fairly common due to the great number of people abused emotionally and physically in their past or present lives. As we minister to them by listening to them and praying for them, we can help them understand Jesus' identification with them in their suffering. In ministering to both of these groups of forgotten people, the writer to the Hebrews urges us to put ourselves in their place as prisoners and victims. This requires more than a shallow momentary sympathy. Jesus would have us experience an empathetic union with them as we actually feel their feelings as they face their situation and suffering. This will bring reality and compassion to our ministry to them.

In addition to this advice about ministry to prisoners and victims, we should also remember John 5:19, "The Son can only do what he sees the Father is doing." Whereas many Christians have the problem of indifference and unwillingness to minister, others have the problem of trying to respond to every need in ministry. These sincere people soon find themselves burned out because of trying to minister to every need they see. A friend once said, "Every call on the phone is not necessarily a call from God." We need the discernment of the Holy Spirit to see which of the many needs God wants us to personally respond to.

THE CALL TO COMMITMENT

The gifts of the Spirit are adornments to our Christian life, adornments of a loving God to His bride. They are important and precious, but peripheral. That is, they are not the main means of Christian living. Too many Christians today focus on a cosmetic view of Christianity in which they see themselves in self-improvement programs. Come to Jesus and get your marriage fixed. Come to Jesus and become prosperous. Come to Jesus and get this or that blessing or whatever thing they are looking for. We emphasize strongly to come to Jesus because He is worthy to be worshipped, whether or not He fixes our marriages or heals our bodies or gives us new cars. We may go through life with a marriage partner who for one reason or another is never going to come to Christ or relate in a proper way, but Jesus is still worthy of our loyalty.

The commitment call to Christ is also to the community of Christ, the Church. This means we must learn to love the people we wouldn't necessary even like. This means learning to relate in community with people in a variety of settings: everything from living together in small groups to living independent of one another but interacting as community once, twice or three times a week in meetings and personal relationships.

Acts 2:42 reads, *"They devoted themselves to the Apostles' teaching and to the fellowship, to the breaking of bread and to prayer. Everyone was filled with awe and many wonders and miraculous signs were done by the Apostles. All the believers were together and had everything in common. Selling their possessions and giving to anyone as he had need."*

FOUR CHARACTERISTICS OF HEALTH

A revived and healthy church will have four characteristics: house, hospital, school and army. As a house, we fellowship together as a family. We value relationships and accountability with one another.

As a hospital, we yearn to provide healing and restoration for those who have been wounded. Specifically, we must become skilled in our helping ministries and lift our level of understanding, training, and methodology and pray for more anointing and power as it relates to Scripture and the Holy Spirit's work among us.

As a school, we are committed to equipping the Body of Christ and empowering every member for ministry. Furthermore, unless we educate the pastoral and lay leadership in our churches about the nature of these kinds of problems, we will be speaking to the wrong issues.

As an army, we are committed to benevolence, evangelism and taking the Kingdom of God into the community around us. John Wesley said, "Making an open stand against all the ungodliness and unrighteousness which over-spread our land as a flood is one of the noblest ways of confessing Christ in the face of His enemies."

RELEASING PEOPLE TO "PLAY"

A key passage to understanding God's purpose of every Christian being a minister is 1 Peter 2:9: "But you are a chosen people, a royal priesthood, a holy nation, a people belonging to God, that you may declare the praises of him who called you out or darkness into his wonderful light." All Christians, not just professional ministers, are chosen people, just as Israel was in the Old Testament. As royal priests, we reflect the holiness of God and that of our High Priest, Jesus [Hebrews

7:24; 10:10], offer spiritual sacrifices, intercede for man before God and represent God before man.

Spiritual priesthood means at least three things for effective ministry. **First, all believers have direct access to God** [Hebrews 4:16]. Each believer can speak to God and can hear from God. Overemphasizing our personal relationship with God, however, may lead to excessive individualism. There are those who believe that because they are priests themselves they don't need the rest of the Body of Christ. But the passage in 1 Peter 2:9 says that we are a "priesthood," not priests. That is, as we individually enter into Christ's priesthood, we function corporately as priests. So I don't think it is possible to grow in our priesthood apart from brothers and sisters. We have been called to commit ourselves to a local body of believers and grow with them and in them as one of them.

Second, all believers are priests to each other. We are a community of priests; therefore, we are to serve one another. Again and again in the New Testament we find the admonition to serve and care for one another. This is why the pathway to Christian maturity is marked by becoming more concerned for others than ourselves.

Third, all believers are priests to the world. The job of a priest is to represent God to the people and the people to God. We are bridge builders. Too often the people who are to be a bridge between the community of the unsaved and the God we serve have instead become a barrier. Rather than being a simple organism of life in the world today, we have become an organization that is often impenetrable to non-Christians.

As a holy nation, we are called together to overcome Satan's kingdom. As a people belonging to God, we no longer have personal rights; our lives belong wholly to God. Every believer has been called to minister.

All too often Christians expect their pastors to emulate secular helping professions. We expect medical doctors to treat us, not to train us to treat others. We expect lawyers to advise us, not to train us to solve our legal problems. Hence, we expect pastors to serve us and not train us to do the work of the ministry. But the biblical model of a pastor is more of a player-coach in which pastoral leaders are to teach people to minister over against doing the ministry for the people.

In our church we do not view the paid professional staff as the ones who do all the ministry. The staff's job is to train other people to minister. As they are trained and released to minister, they in turn train others, and the progression is endless and very effective.

The best way for pastoral leaders to begin equipping and training others is to be accessible, visible and vulnerable, to be one of the people in my church who is ministering alongside of me. They lead small groups, pray for the sick, council and so on. Yet many pastors are insecure about the effectiveness of their work and thus try to protect themselves by not releasing the church to minister.

At the church I pastor, we also try to avoid using titles and positions. That is why I have adopted phrases like, "an elder is an elder to the degree that he elds." This is a humorous way of communicating a truth that eldership is not a position to be attained but a function to be performed. Many people have the title without the reality. I want to focus on the reality, which is learning to minister and serve others. That's what it looks like to be in a church family to me.

RELEASING SPIRITUAL GIFTS

The release and practice of spiritual gifts is another important part of equipping everyone to minister. Many Christians believe in spiritual gifts but do not practice them. But if we don't use them, the gifts are of no value. There are several ways in which the Church can help everyone minister in the gifts more effectively.

The first way is by the laying on of hands for impartation. This is referenced by Paul in 2 Timothy 1:6 where he tells Timothy to "fan into flame the gift of God, which is in you through the laying on of my hands." If this has happened to you, recognize that the laying on of hands is where the process starts, and a number of years may go by while the gift is developed in you. This time of training is normal. If you are to give to others, you must first receive from God that which you are to give, and sometimes that takes some time. 2 Timothy 2:6 tells us, "The hard working farmer should be the first to receive a share of the crops."

Paul of Tarsus waited thirteen years after Ananias laid hands on him before he ministered significantly, and that was after receiving several confirmations of his ministry. Some of you have had false starts. Don't become discouraged and quit. Wait. Get ratification from the leaders in your church of this calling. Walk with the Lord for awhile. Learn to be faithful in little things. You don't want to go on your own zeal and beget an Ishmael. Wait for Isaac, your ministry of promise.

Second, the Church needs to leave room for people to learn to do the works of the Father, a place where people can experiment, a place to succeed and fail. A safe place should be provided within a local church for the believer to learn how to prophesy, to heal the sick and to minister in evangelism. The Apostles had a safe place with Jesus. First they watched Him minister. Next they ministered while He watched. Finally they ministered on their own. It took time for them to learn.

Part of making room means taking people along with us and showing them, taking them by the hand and saying, "You've seen me pray for people, now you pray." If your church is too large to accommodate this type of learning, you probably need to break it down into smaller units for equipping. New Christians need to be trained and cared for, "so that the Body of Christ may be built up until we all reach unity in the faith and in the knowledge of the Son of God and become mature, attaining to the whole measure of the fullness of Christ" [Ephesians 4:12b, 13].

Third, contemporary churches are often built on a present day corporation style model of leadership rather than a Spirit-led model. The Spirit-led church chooses its leaders according to gifts, character and ministries, recognizing the work of the Spirit in the individual's life. The institutionalized church too often chooses its leaders according to the position they have in the secular community. That's not entirely wrong, because in the church there are certain kinds of administrative work for which one needs technical skills, but most of the work of ministry needs to be done according to a spiritual model. If I need computer work done, it isn't necessary that the worker be proficient at praying for the sick; it's better for the job if he or she had computer training. But if the worker is going to work closely with the rest of the office staff, it is very helpful for him or her not only to be a believer, but also to have the same basic philosophy and values as the rest of the church.

LIBERATING WOMEN FOR MINISTRY

Another key for releasing many to ministry is giving particular atten-tion to releasing women in ministry. There are some foundational truths that serve as a plumb line for answering the question concerning women's ministry in the church. Genesis 1:26-27 tells us that men and women were created in the image of God. For God's glory to be expressed in humanity, both the partnership of male and female and their community together are needed. God intended a complementary relationship between man and woman, one marked by equality in per-sonhood and mutual submission. Keep in mind that since the fall of humankind there has always been the problem of people enslaving one another. Today, when we deal with the biblical perspective of releasing and freeing people, we need to recognize that all men and women are enslaved at various levels of life, and we all need to be freed from the things that hold us back from being all that we can be.

Remember, God created Eve as a suitable helper, one corresponding to Adam. The implied relationship is best expressed by the word "com-plementary." But their harmonious relationship was undercut by the fall in which man became a ruler over the woman. But Jesus' victory at the cross has overcome the results of the fall. As a result, the princi-ple for all relationships in the Body of Christ is mutual submis-sion and service, that is, to show preference toward one another.

The principle for all relationships in the body of Christ is mutual submission and service, that is, to show preference toward one another.

The clearest proclamation of the position of women is given by Paul in Galatians 3:28: "There is nei-ther Jew, nor Greek, slave nor free, male nor female, for you are all one in Christ Jesus." The context of this passage is that both men and women have free access to the eternal life and the Kingdom of God. With the coming of Christ, we see women being related to in a whole new way. They no longer were treated as property, as chattel. Jesus elevated their position. Women should be operating shoulder to shoulder with men, not with female dominance, not male dominance, but Christ dominance.

Because of the position of priesthood that God gives to each and every believer—whether male or female, young or old, smart or not—every Christian is called to minister. God gives good gifts to equip his ministers. He calls for the Church to be a place where ministry can happen, where non-Christians can see the works and life of Jesus being lived out. Let's be about God's business!

DEVOTED TO COMMUNITY

Amazing things were happening in those first few days of Christianity. Thousands were converted in a day. Miracles were happening. The followers of Jesus—in direct conflict with the authorities—proclaimed the resurrection of Jesus, the Christ. Those early Christians learned some sobering lessons through the deaths of Ananias and Sapphira (God's discipline), the martyrdom of Stephen (total commitment) and the dispersion of the Church (no earthly security).

How did the followers of Jesus cope? Acts 2:42 gives us a glimpse of community life as it was in that day even in the midst of incredible upheaval, including spiritual revival: "They devoted themselves to the apostles' teaching and to the fellowship, to the breaking of bread."

Why didn't they devote themselves to the Apostles' signs? Why didn't they just meet to have more experiences? Because they were under the wisdom of God; they were under the tutelage of the Scripture. These converts came out of Judaism and had been taught the Word since childhood. They had a grasp of the Word and it's importance. So their devotion was focused on the Word of God! We leave room for the phenomena, and we've asked the Holy Spirit to come, but we've never taken the focus off the Word of God because we want to emulate the first Christians in Jerusalem: "They devoted themselves to the Apostles' teaching..."

Being devoted to one another involves deepening your prayer life and fellowship. It means deepening your commitment and interdependence on one another. If revival doesn't result in these behaviors—giving to the poor and sharing our faith—is it truly revival? They were as devoted to being a community as they were to their own personal growth.

Let's become like these people....devoted.

Nine

EVANGELISM: WHY WE MUST DO IT

"THE MEAT IS IN THE STREET"

The Bible regularly uses the metaphors of fishing and farming to explain evangelism. Remember, Jesus wasn't talking to people who went fishing on weekends or enjoyed a good bass tournament. He was speaking to men whose survival depended on catching fish. If the fisherman didn't catch fish on any one day, his family went hungry. Jesus' kind of fishing meant catching fish.

The people hearing Jesus clearly understood this. Jesus likened evangelism to being "fishers of men," and He meant exactly what He said: catching people for the Kingdom. Jesus used the metaphor to express His heart that fishing must mean catching.

Jesus also spoke of farming as a metaphor for evangelism. Again, Jesus was speaking to professional farmers. These weren't people who kept a small vegetable garden in the backyard as a hobby. These were people whose very lives depended on bringing in a harvest. Jesus spoke of evangelism as fishing to emphasize the catching and farming to emphasize the harvest that would soon come. The metaphors imply an objective standard for measuring success: the number and quality of fish caught, or the amount and quality of crop harvested.

If you asked a commercial fisherman on the Sea of Galilee if he had a good day, you wouldn't hear, "Yes, you should have seen how far I threw the net. And I'm really getting good at standing up in the boat." No, his answer would be to point to his catch. Many fish equals a good day. Jesus meant for us to catch and harvest many people with the Good News of the Kingdom of God.

The goal of evangelism is not only the creation of individual disciples of Jesus; it also includes building bodies of people, the Body of Christ. God created us for fellowship. Right relationships are a part of God's plan for our lives. Because of this corporate, or social dimension, God frequently brings clusters of people to His Kingdom all at one time. Many times we focus too much on individuals, forgetting that when one member of a family or social grouping is affected, it can result in a whole family being won.

After healing the demon-possessed man in the region of the

Gerasenes, Jesus told him, "Go home to your family and tell them how much the Lord has done for you, and how he had had mercy on you" (Mark 5:19). He "went away and began to tell in the Decapolis how much Jesus had done for him. And all the people were amazed" (5:20). A similar incident occurs with the Samaritan woman after her encounter with Jesus (John 4:28-30, 39-42).

We also read of a royal official from Capernaum whose whole household was saved through power evangelism (John 4:46-53). He came seeking Jesus, asking Him to heal his son. After rebuking the official for needing to "see miraculous signs and wonders" to believe, Jesus healed his son. What is unique about this miracle is that Jesus did not lay hands on the boy and pray over him. He simply declared the miracle done and told the official to go home; his son was healed. In response to the supernatural meeting of the official's need, "he and all his household believed."

In Acts 16, the Philippian jailer was saved after "the foundations of the prison were shaken," the prison doors flew open and all the prisoners' chains came loose—including Paul and Silas'. After hearing the Gospel, he believed. At the end of the evening, the jailor "was filled with joy because he had come to believe in God—he and his whole family" (Acts 16:34).

EMPOWERED CHRISTIANS

A recent study indicates that 86 percent of all Christians came to a saving faith in Jesus through the testimony of a friend or relative. Advertising, pastoral visits and organized evangelistic outreaches accounted for only 14 percent! We shouldn't be surprised about these statistics because this was exactly how Jesus planned it.

In Matthew 28:19-20, Jesus commissioned the disciples to, "Go and make disciples of all nations...teaching them to obey everything I have commanded you." In this, the Great Commission, God called every individual believer to reproduce in others what God has done for and in them—we are to spread the Good News that Jesus has died on the cross to forgive sins and give eternal life!

The Great Commission would be an overwhelming task if not for two important sources of power. First, the Gospel itself has intrinsic power, the power to persuade and save. Paul writes, "I am not ashamed of the gospel, because it is the power of God for the salvation of everyone who believes" (Romans 1:16). The message of the Cross penetrates hearts, overcomes fears and defeats unbelief!

The second source of power is the Holy Spirit. In His last post-resurrection appearance to the disciples, Jesus instructed them to "wait for the gift my Father promised" [Holy Spirit] in order to "receive power" and "be my witnesses in Jerusalem, and in all Judea and Samaria, and the ends of the earth" (Acts 1:4,5,8). On Pentecost the Spirit came, and 3,000 were added to the Church, so our message has power, and we are empowered messengers!

God has arranged it so that we are the only Bible that some people will ever hear. If we proclaim the message of the Cross in the power of the Spirit, Jesus will do the rest. Paul wrote, "You show that you are a letter from Christ, the result of our ministry, written not with ink but with the Spirit of the living God, not on tablets of stone, but on tablets of human hearts" (2 Corinthians 3:3). Spiritual growth is important not only for our own benefit, but also for the benefit of others who will be changed through the message we carry.

THE MESSAGE WE CARRY

We have record of Paul sharing his salvation testimony two times in Acts in hostile settings, even though Acts is a very selective book (Acts 22:3-18 & 26:9-18). Paul shared first his "before" story, then the two most important questions, "Who are you, Lord?" and "What shall I do, Lord?" and then he finished with God's purpose for him.

Several other times Paul alluded to his testimony in his teaching to the Church, always in the context of the amazing grace and vast mercy of God that led to his response of total commitment:

1. 1 Corinthians 15:9-10, "Because I persecuted the church of God...but by the grace of God I am..."

2. Galatians 1:13-16, "For you have heard of my former manner of

life in Judaism...called me through His grace, and was pleased to reveal His Son in me, that I might preach..."

3. Philippians 3:4-11, "If anyone else has a mind to put confidence in the flesh, I far more...But whatever things were gain to me, I counted as loss..."

4. 2 Timothy 1:12-17, "I thank Christ Jesus our Lord, who...even though I was formally...BUT the grace of our Lord..."

Again and again Paul shared his story, where he had come from and, by the grace of God, what Christ had done in him and was doing through him. Sometimes we don't realize that in just remembering where we came from before Christ, and in sharing with others, the impact we will have on those around us. We are to constantly share our story wherever we are to whomever we come in contact with, just as Paul did.

WHY WE SHARE WITH OTHERS

There are both temporal and eternal rewards for sharing our faith with others. Again and again Scripture fills us with the hope of knowing Jesus Christ, but what about the hope and excitement we feel when we share with others? Let's take a look at what Scripture tells us about what happens when we follow Christ but also, as believers, what we are called to share with others. Every time I share the Gospel with others, it is the most exciting part of my time on this earth, for when we are no longer here, we will no longer have the reward of taking part in sharing about Christ with those around us.

There are temporal rewards the Scripture talks about:
· Ephesians 3:18-19—To know by personal experience a love which is beyond knowing
· 1 Peter 1:8—To be filled with a joy, which cannot be expressed, the next thing to glory!
· Philippians 4:7—To have our hearts guarded by a peace, which transcends all understanding!

There are also some eternal rewards: "I have fought the good fight, I have finished the race, I have kept the faith. Now there is in store for me the crown of righteousness which the Lord, the righteous Judge, will award to me on that day- and not only to me, but also to all who have longed for His appearing" (2 Timothy 4:7-8).

DON'T BE INTIMIDATED

In Acts 19, we find Paul going into the various communities preaching the Gospel and each time encountering demonic strongholds. At this time Ephesus was no little country village; it probably had something in excess of 500,000 people living there at the time when Paul arrived. It was a major marketplace, and the agora, the mall of Ephesus, would have accommodated around 40,000 people just in this one area. This was not a slowly moving area but rather a very fast moving one. Paul meets up with Apollos and has to update and teach to bring the people into a full understanding of Christ.

The fourth verse is where we find Paul finding a small group of people that he ministers to by leading them to Christ and baptizing them. They're now prophesying and believing. But remember the community that he's in: the unsaved are everywhere, and there are false gods everywhere. And still Paul goes in and persuasively speaks about the Kingdom of God. The message is always about the Kingdom of God.

We often look at everything around and feel ourselves becoming overwhelmed! All the people, all the busyness, and it all can look too scary at times. But here Paul gives us a great example of not being intimidated. Paul could have arrived and said, "Oh these people are too far gone; they worship everyone and everything, and they're never going to listen to me." But instead Paul did as he usually did, and he spoke with boldness and with the sincerity of the Gospel.

Don't look around you and be fearful that no one will take you seriously; be bold, be brave and remember that you are to be witnesses of the Kingdom of the almighty God! If the people don't listen, shake it off and move on to the people that will. I guarantee there are those who are waiting and willing to listen.

Acts 19:8-9a: "Paul entered the synagogue and spoke boldly there for three months, arguing persuasively about the kingdom of God. But some of them became obstinate; they refused to believe and publicly maligned the Way. So Paul left them…"

THE POWER OF KINDNESS

"I'm pro-life," said Norma McCorvey, the Jane Roe in the Supreme Court's 1973 Roe vs. Wade decision legalizing abortion and, for more than two decades, a symbol of the abortion-rights movement.

McCorvey's decision to quit her job as marketing director for a Dallas abortion clinic came after her conversion to Christianity. "I think abortion's wrong. I think what I did with Roe vs. Wade was wrong," she said in a radio interview in Dallas. McCorvey said she recently became emotional after seeing empty swings in a park, thinking there were no children because, "they've all been aborted."

McCorvey, a recovering alcoholic, taunted Phillip "Flip" Benham, president of Operation Rescue, when OR moved its offices next door to her clinic. McCorvey and Benham, who is the same age, 47, and also is a recovering alcoholic, formed a close friendship during lulls in clinic appointments. Benham, who is a minister, baptized McCorvey in a swimming pool at a private ceremony. "Jesus Christ has reached through the abortion mill wall and touched the heart of Norma McCorvey," he said. McCorvey's 1994 autobiography, I am Roe: My life, Roe v. Wade, and Freedom of Choice, reveals that she is a lesbian. It details her difficult life, which has included drug abuse, being raped while a teenager and a failed marriage.

Benham's kindness in the face of taunts from McCovery shows the depth of his compassion for the lost. "He won her over, not with harsh rhetoric, but by treating her as a valuable person." Is there a lesson here for those pro-lifers who believe confrontation, even violence, is the only way to stop abortion? One hardens hearts; the other can change lives."

[Excerpt taken from *Vineyard Reflections*, 1995 From National & International Religion Report]

WHAT ABOUT HARDSHIP AND DEATH?

"I'M GOIN' TO HEAVEN! WILL I SEE YOU THERE?"

When dealing with life's uncertainties, two erroneous teachings take on the appearance of being biblical mysteries. Christians who confuse these mistaken views for biblical truths actually intensify their suffering.

First, some mistakenly believe that all Christians are protected from calamity, hardship, pain and loss. Because God is with them, they reason, their lives will turn out according to their expectations. Secondly, some believe that Christians never struggle. And if they do, it is because they're not exercising the quality of faith they ought to for those circumstances. People with this belief system see themselves as sinning if they have periods of disillusionment and despair.

Frankly, if those ideas are true, then I'm not a Christian at all. Not only have I suffered physically with health problems, but I also spent a great deal of time struggling with depression during my battle with cancer. Most of you can probably call to mind dozens of occasions when you've felt less than victorious in your approach to a hard time. You're in good company.

Trials and testing seem to be a normal part of the Christian life. Our job is to be ready and able to handle the tests with God's help, secure in the knowledge of His care and ultimate delivery.

One night, years ago, I awoke with a jolt. "What is it Lord?"

Something in my spirit wasn't right. As the father of four married children and a grandfather, my immediate thoughts were, "Is it one of the kids? Grandkids?"

No, that wasn't it. It was something else. My mouth felt dry. I had the distinct impression from the Lord that something frightening was headed my way. Slipping out of bed, I retreated to my prayer corner in the living room and prayed my favorite crises prayer: "Oh God, Oh God." I opened the Bible, expecting the Lord to not only comfort me, but to reveal the nature of this dire warning. He led me to Psalm 33. I read verse 18: "But the eyes of the Lord are on those who fear him, on those whose hope is in his unfailing love."

The second half of the verse perplexed me: "...to deliver them from death and keep them alive in famine."

"I'm certainly not starving," I thought at the time; I weighed more than enough, and I didn't think I was going to die. I read the rest of the Psalm: "We wait in hope for the Lord: he is our help and our shield."

I relaxed and let out a sigh. I was relieved to be reminded that God was in charge, and He certainly made that clear to me once again. Seven days later, the doctor told me I had cancer.

When I began radiation treatments for the cancer, I discovered what it was like to walk through the "valley of the shadow of death." As I went weeks without eating solid foods, I began to realize the physical and emotional trauma could no way be walked out unless I took the hand of the Lord and walked with Him.

Even so, being led in such a season with such uncertainties that keep you alert to every changing scenario, I began to cling to every nuance of the doctor's words, shrugs and grimaces and experienced the full range of emotions that come with a life-threatening illness. I wept as I saw my utter need to go deeper in God. I had to embrace the truth that I could not control or plan my life.

Some Christians believe we will never struggle with feelings of doubt, fear, anxiety, disillusionment, sorrow, agony and in fact believe those feelings are sin. That has not been my experience as a Christian. There are struggles, but one thing I also found was that the view of the valley gave me a focus on Christ that I wouldn't have gained any other way.

Stars shine brighter in the desert. There are no obstructions, no distractions, no competing lights. The view from the valley isn't so bad because Jesus shines so clearly. I knew He was there, even when I didn't always feel close to Him. During that year of treatment, my wife, Carol, and I made trips to the hospital together. It was in the radiation treatment room where I experienced God's peace transcending my understanding.

In the waiting room there are all sorts of people fighting cancer, many that were worse off than I was. Some had smoking-related cancer where they were missing parts of their faces. In the first few days I was so overwhelmed by the misery of the people that was in that room that I shrank into myself. I couldn't do anything or talk to anyone. I didn't want to talk to anyone.

But as Carol and I became aware of God's presence in that dire situation, the Holy Spirit began drawing me out. We became aware that the sharing of the Word at the appropriate time could move others around us toward Christ. Sometimes our experiences don't fit our understanding of what the Bible teaches. On one hand, we believe that God is sovereign and that He sent Jesus to commission us to pray for healing. And on the other hand, we know from experience that healing doesn't always take place. Why would God command us to heal the sick and then choose not to back up our act [so to speak]?

It can be downright discouraging as I learned years ago in my own congregation when I began to teach on healing. It was nine months before we saw the first person healed. The temptation was to withdraw from practicing Christ's commands or, at the other extreme, to drum up a false bravado to convince God to do what we thought He ought to do. Neither posture is correct.

Our part is to obey His commands and know His will; it is given in the Bible. Still, the Bible doesn't tell us which people God will heal or not heal, and God has the sovereign choice concerning each person for whom we pray. Will He heal, or will He extend the grace for suffering instead? Or will He grant healing at a later time? These very real issues leave us where we began: trusting God to make the sovereign choices for our lives.

These very real issues leave us where we began: trusting God to make the sovereign choices for our lives.

Over the years I've prayed for many that were healed and many that were not including those that were my friends. I remember when I was speaking in South Africa at a large conference I was asked to go to a home of a lady that was dying of cancer. She was emaciated, weighing only 85 pounds. She had been sent home to die. Her body was full of cancer. We prayed for her, and honestly, not with a lot of fervency: in fact I really felt nothing.

That night she woke up with a vibrant tingling feeling through out her body, and for the next four hours her body was full of intense heat. She tried to call out to her husband who was in the next room but couldn't raise her voice loud enough for him to hear. Alone and frightened, she crawled back into the bathroom, her body racked with pain. At the time she thought, "O my God, my body is coming apart, and I'm dying!" Without knowing it, she eliminated from her body a large number of tumors and then fell back to sleep. She didn't know if she'd wake up, but half an hour later she woke up feeling incredibly refreshed.

Later her husband woke up to the smell of freshly brewed coffee. "What are you doing?" he asked, astonished to see his wife on her feet and preparing breakfast. She replied with sudden understanding, "God has healed me!" Two days later her doctors gave her a clean bill of health! The doctors couldn't find any cancer in her body. Without much energy to pray on our part and without any desperation or faith on her part, the Lord chose to heal this women's cancer-infested body through His divine means. That's God, and that is sometimes how He does it.

When I was being treated for cancer, someone wrote me a letter asking, "Do you still believe in healing now that you've got cancer?" I wrote back "Yes! Of course I do." And that is the truth; but I also believe in pain. Both are found in the Word of God. In the year I spent battling cancer, God purged me of a lot of bad habits and attitudes that weren't right, and through it I grew stronger as a Christian. Some of my greatest advances in spiritual maturity came as I embraced the pain, as each day I had to choose to allow God to accomplish His work in me by any method, even adversity.

But going through pain and suffering should not frighten us. God is sovereign, and He alone is our refuge, our resource and our peace.

LIFE'S PAINFUL LOSSES

It's not what you have, but instead what has you. Several years ago, two people in our church really desired to have a baby. Time and time again we had laid hands on those that were unable to conceive for whatever reason and saw them deliver babies a year or two later. This happened over and over again all over the world! But for these two people in our church, pregnancy did not come easily. They waited for years for their prayers to be answered. One day, it was prophesied that they would indeed have a child, and they became pregnant following the prophecy.

Imagine their elation seeing their baby boy born after so much waiting! This little boy was named after my brother-in-law and me and brought joy to all of us who knew his family. Three short years later, this little longed-for boy died suddenly of a mysterious infection. What a shock!

The Lord saw fit to take him home almost overnight. At this point, one might conjecture all kinds of reasons why, but the truth is, we don't really know why. All we can affirm and remember is that God is good and kind and just. Someday, when the family and he are together again, we will know that God's decision was good and kind and just, though it doesn't feel like it at the time.

Not every testing is a negative testing. It isn't always some dreadful thought, deed or misfortune. Sometimes the tests come in the form of blessing.

> **All we can affirm and remember is that God is good and kind and just.**

Some of the most difficult tests I've watched Christians go through are to some degree the result of God's blessing. All of the sudden, some of these brothers and sisters have great access to popularity, visibility or wealth.

In fact, I believe that it's not the stripping of wealth that is the most difficult test, but the acquiring of it. It can propel a believer into a world that is heady and powerful. I've seen it produce some very un-Christlike qualities in the lives of individuals being tested.

That's why outward obedience is not enough. If you haven't surrendered your life in total to the Lord, you will be vulnerable to shifts in circumstances and emotions. Those things can conspire to undermine your determination to "do" for God. Instead, you may find that your inner person is waiting for an opportunity to assert its unregenerate self instead of fulfilling the habit of obedience born in love. You see, in my opinion, it's not what you have, but what has you.

HEROES WHO DOUBT

In the first twenty-eight verses of Hebrews 11, which exploit the details of many biblical heroes, we look at their hardship and their experiences of doubt, confusion and how they most certainly did not rise to every occasion.

Sarah laughed when God promised her a son in her old age. Joseph lorded God's promise of greatness to him over his brothers, causing them to despise him. David used his powerful position to commit adultery and murder, yet he is called a man after God's own heart. The Scripture calls these heroes great men and women of faith. God fulfilled His purposes through them in spite of their weaknesses and because of their obedience.

The mystery that moves us to worship our sovereign God is that He operates with you and me today in the same way. God uses mere people to accomplish His divine purposes. None of us is required to be super human. Instead, we are to remember that He is God and we are not.

Hebrews 11 removes any illusions that our lives in God are safeguarded from evil, trials or hardships. In fact, this chapter might lead us to think that trouble actually follows the faithful of God. Beginning in verse 35, the author mentions unknown men and women of God who were unwilling to recant their faith.

Interestingly enough, the twentieth century has seen more people martyred for their faith than the previous nineteen centuries. People around the world today are dying for their testimony in Christ. They are willing to do so because they are steadfastly committed to looking beyond the immediate prospect of death. God promises one conclusion to this life: His eternal home, which has no tears or sorrow.

If the greatness of faith is based on never having painful or frightening experiences and never having doubtful thoughts, then these people could not be viewed as those who exercised faith.

WHAT'S THE WORST THAT CAN HAPPEN?

When all is said and done, dying is the last, worst thing that any of us will face. As Christians, however, we need to recognize that it's also the best thing. Going to heaven is what we signed up for. That's not so bad, is it?

Isn't that why you became a Christian? It was for me.

Recognizing and reaffirming that death no longer has the final power over you goes a long way in defusing the anxiety bomb.

Almighty God is the Lord over all, and He orders the affairs of men. If He chooses to take your loved one, it's something that you cannot overrule. There are seasons and times in which God chooses to do things that seem contrary to what we believe His will toward us ought to be. By accepting the tension between what we know and what we don't know yet, we can begin to let go of the anxiety.

A day is coming when the things that are now fuzzy and hard to understand will be made clear to us. We will know even as we are known (1 Corinthians 13:12). Until then, it is our job to live with the uncertainty of the outcomes in this life since we have a secure hope in our eternal destination. This understanding is the key to embracing pain, hardship, loss and trials in life.

Eleven

WHAT IS BIBLICAL
LEADERSHIP?

"SHOW ME YOUR PUPPIES,
AND I'LL GIVE YOU YOUR PAPERS."

I believe it's important to correct the misunderstanding regarding John's beliefs about the "Women in Ministry" subject. It has been inferred in various articles and teachings that John would not allow women leaders to pastor the churches. That really isn't true. Let me try to explain our thoughts, where we were coming from. You have to understand, first of all, that John and I were Quakers—evangelical Quakers—and as Quakers, deep down in our bones we didn't think or look at Christians according to gender. We saw individuals as parts of the Body of Christ, and it was not up to us to appoint leaders, pastors, preachers, teachers, etc. to their place in the Body. That was a function of the Holy Spirit, and all we could do was recognize what the Spirit was doing and who the Spirit was using. It's an old Quaker thing that we call Recording. God is "using" someone (male or female) in some function of the Church, and we recognize that fact, and we write it down! Simple, huh?

It sounded ludicrous to us when women (or men) wanted to be ordained to the ministry when it was our understanding that there was only one ministry, the ministry of Jesus into which we are all ordained. John's answer was always, "Show me your puppies, and I'll give you the papers." His meaning: let me first see what God has done and how the Holy Spirit is using you before we give you a badge defining your place in the Body of Christ. And if a woman (or man) thinks having a title somehow releases the flow of the Holy Spirit, that woman (or man) has misunderstood how it works.

The Holy Spirit is the head of the Church, and He will use us how He pleases, and we should be happy about that because a church administered by the Spirit of God is a beautiful thing.

Our son and daughter-in-law, Sean and Christy Wimber, have planted a Vineyard in the heart of Yorba Linda. (Although John could-

149

n't be here to see it, I know he is a part of it.) Christy is the "senior pastor," and she does the teaching. Sean does the sound and leads the men's stuff, and they both go about looking and finding who Jesus is using and putting them in their place in the Body of Christ. Long before the new Vineyard even started, puppies were filling up their house and spilling out the windows. We gave them the papers! That is what John believed in.

Thank you for allowing me to give you another way to understand John Wimber.

- Carol Wimber

KEEP TELLING THE STORIES

It's important as leaders that we ask ourselves the question, "Why am I here?" We have a record of the Apostle Paul sharing his salvation testimony two times in Acts in hostile settings. Paul shared the "before" of his conversion story, then the answers to the two most important questions, "Who are you Lord?" and "What shall I do, Lord?" Several other times Paul alluded to his testimony through his teaching to the Church, and it was always in the context of the amazing grace and vast mercy of God that led to his response of total commitment.

First, we must remember to constantly tell our story. Why am I here? What am I doing? What are some of the things God has called me to do to serve His purposes? [Luke 14:17-18; Matthew 10:7-8; 24:14; Acts 20:24].

Remembering why you do what you do is most important for the whole of the race.

Why do you do what you do? Why did you choose to follow through with the call you believe God has on your life? Remembering why you do what you do is most important for the whole of the race.

Second, we are called to continually tell His story [1 Corinthians 1:15-18], revealing who the Father is, our inheritance, our birthright in Christ, how He is the creator of all things, the sustainer of it all, the head of the Church, the one chosen to give Himself in order that we may live.

The power in the story you continue to tell is the most powerful story ever taught! I don't quite get it when pastors say they have run out of messages; I mean, the power in the "main and the plain" of the Scriptures themselves never gets old, never gets to the place where we can wear those stories out. Keep telling the story! Keep on telling all the things Christ has done on our behalf!

GUIDED BY THE SPIRIT

What is your model of leadership? Where does it come from? Is it biblical? Many Christian leaders work off a model that views the leader as chief executive officer. He sets goals, makes plans based on the best available data, strategizes and in general takes a no-nonsense approach.

Church leaders also tend to view themselves as professionals. The leader is seen as someone who has accumulated a lot of knowledge about Christianity.

Both these models frequently lead to some success. I have come to believe, however, that neither is suitable as the fundamental approach to leadership in the Church. There's nothing wrong with managerial planning and professional competence per se. Unfortunately, though, we often allow these tools to exclude dependence on the Lord Jesus Christ and the guidance of His Spirit.

> In the New Testament, a leader is distinguished not so much by administrative skills as by ability to pass on the way of life he has been taught, not so much by what he knows as by whom he knows.

The New Testament model of leadership is different in many respects from these models. It is essentially concerned with personally following a master—ultimately, the Master. In the New Testament, a leader is distinguished not so much by administrative skills as by ability to pass on the way of life he has been taught, not so much by what he knows as by whom he knows. His skills and knowledge spring from his relationship with God and a human teacher and result in a changed character, marked by humility, wisdom and discernment.

The Church has tried to marry this New Testament model of leadership with the corporate/professional models. The marriage hasn't worked too well; we pay homage to humility while discarding constant dependence on the Master. Primary reliance on professional management tools replaces reliance on the Lord's personal presence and guidance through His Spirit. We no longer expect His action and direction.

Planning...After God Speaks

I'm no stranger to corporate planning. For years I've been involved in the church growth movement, which has contributed much to the technical understanding of how to run a church. I have designed five and ten-year master plans for Christian organizations. I am familiar with the process of sorting ideas, establishing goals, putting plans down on paper and helping people to advance. I am not against planning. I am in favor of planning—after God speaks.

God wants to speak. The challenge lies not in getting God to guide us but in waiting on Him faithfully in order to hear Him.

At the Vineyard we have experienced discernment regarding where geographically to focus our efforts, what goals to set for growth, how to arrange pastoral structures, when to hold major events and similar matters. I do not believe that this is anything that other churches and groups should not also expect to experience.

To give an example, I believe the Lord holds back numerical growth in favor of growth in character and holiness. Back in 1989 we had around 1,200 new people come into the church, which is a good growth year for a congregation of 7,500. But the Holy Spirit showed me that in 1990 we would see little numerical growth. Instead we would see significant things going on in people's lives—the kinds of challenges and activities that usually result in a higher level of perseverance and a more solid commitment. I told the staff to prepare for it, and starting in January of 1990 we did see a decline in the number of new people coming into the church. There was a shift in what was going on in the lives of many of the leaders and other members.

We also receive discernment for outreach activities. The Lord will give us sensitivity to some place or group of people, indicating that we are to go here or there, work with this age group or use one kind of deployment rather than another kind. As a staff, we could sense that this was the next move for our church, and we made a choice to unite in taking it on together.

These decisions all involve the use of discernment-type gifts. We call this loosely, "the eyes of God" or "the eyes of the Spirit." These are gifts such as the word of wisdom, the word of knowledge, the distinguishing of spirits, prophetic gifts and less often, tongues and interpretation.

Having had these as well as other experiences of guidance, we never plan before God speaks. We often find ourselves like a ship at sea without wind, all our sails sagging. We could at those times develop a plan, but there is no impetus for it. The Spirit of God is not speaking.

I should note that we are not very successful at getting God to speak. There are long periods when we cannot "get anything out of Him," that is, what He is planning. And so we spend a significant amount of time, sometimes months on end, simply seeking the Lord and asking Him to give direction.

PASTORAL CARE

In addition to discernment for the church's corporate life, we have also come to expect discernment about the people we are pastoring. For example, those of us on the pastoral staff often receive a sense from the Lord to ask questions of a member. Even though we have an average attendance of more than 5,000 people, while I am preaching, I often know who is not there. I will come from the pulpit and, while my associates are still with me, list some people: "Check on this family, check on that family." Seeing people in passing, I will sometimes receive discernment about something going on in their lives.

Spiritual insight may concern demonic activity in people's lives. I will sometimes have a sense of which demons are affecting people and what they may be doing in their lives. God gives other spiritual gifts that are significant tools for pastoral care. There are gifts that I would call "the hands of God," which have to do with faith, healing and miracles, and "the voice of God," gifts that have to do with teaching and preaching, tongues, interpretations, prophecy and so on. These operate in conjunction with the gifts of discernment.

GROWING IN DISCERNMENT

Growing in servant leadership according to the New Testament model involves growing in discernment. How can we do this?

In the New Testament, the most commonly disciplined problem in the Church was not immorality but divisiveness, including gossip and the carrying of tales. And so the Scripture is replete with instructions and exhortations about talking charitably. We must discipline ourselves if we are to do this. If we do, we will, as a byproduct, find that the dullness of our spiritual discernment is removed.

Opening ourselves to the Spirit's gifts of discernment also involves housecleaning. Some months ago, for example, the Lord spoke to me out of Psalm 101 about "no unclean thing will pass my eye."

"Lord, what is passing my eye?" I prayed.

I realized it was television. I was not watching a lot of television. But the Spirit of God spoke to me clearly and said to turn the thing off. We did. Within a matter of days, I could sense discernment in my life increasing.

A clean house doesn't necessarily represent a filled home. We must put aside sin in order to pursue God so that the Spirit will fill us and manifest His love through us. We must develop a lifestyle in which we go before the Lord and receive from Him and operate out of that.

Much of our trouble in the Church today relates directly to our lack of heavenly mindedness. As the Apostles often completely missed the significance of Jesus' words right up to the end of His earthly life, we often miss God's purposes. We are oblivious to the ways He wants to work through us and guide us.

But the Apostles advanced from dullness and lack of discernment to a condition of considerable discernment. Consider Acts 5, in which Peter was able to look into the heart of Ananias and Sapphira and see that they had lied to the Holy Spirit. The point here is not the severity of their punishment, but the clarity of Peter's discernment.

Much training of Christian leaders today reflects an exclusion of spiritual acumen or ability. As a result, many of us are operating in a spiritual kingdom without much spiritual discernment. For personal reliance on Christ and the Spirit, we substitute secular arts of leadership. But more is available to the Body of Christ because the Lord Jesus wants to lead us.

Not all of us will have the same giftedness, but corporately the Church can have that same kind of spiritual discernment that we see in Scripture. Our doing so is dependent on our moving away from a worldly focus into the spiritual dimension that is available to every Christian leader to operate in.

APOSTOLIC (STRENGTH IN) WEAKNESS

How do we learn to lead according to the New Testament model of personal dependence on the Master? Unlike the managerial and professional models of leadership, the key is not mastering certain skills or accumulating knowledge. The key is humility—humble character and humble dependence on the Lord.

We must understand that humble servant leadership entails weakness. In our Western world, we see no positive association between weakness and leadership. Neither, at first, did Paul. But after asking the Lord three times to remove the difficulty of the thorn in the flesh, Paul heard God say, "My grace is sufficient for you, for my power is made perfect in weakness." And so Paul wrote, "I will boast all the more gladly about my weaknesses, so that Christ's power may rest in me" [2 Corinthians 1:9].

Frequently, God invites us to accept weakness voluntarily. For instance, we are encouraged to seek God in intercession. For people who like to take charge and make things happen, sustained intercession seems like a very weak activity. Yet, we are all called to this activity. In 1 Thessalonians, Paul tells us, "Night and day we pray most earnestly that we may see you again and supply what is lacking in your faith" [3:10].

Fasting likewise is an activity of weakness. We fast in secret, in our closet. We can increase our fasting and prayer without getting immediate results. They may be stored up for some time later in our lifetimes or in the lifetime of others. We cannot manipulate God through prayer and fasting; we cannot get Him on our timetable. In all these ways, fasting seems like a weak endeavor.

LEADERS WITH A LIMP

Sometime ago I lamented to a respected colleague about my problems. "I've had some real setbacks in my life," I said, "and I run into younger pastors all the time that are struggling with serious problems with profound effects on their lives." He responded with a chagrined laugh, "Well, I don't trust any leader that doesn't walk with a limp."

It brought to mind the imagery of Jacob's arguing with the Lord, who appeared in the form of an angel, at Penile [see Genesis 32:22-23]. Toward the end of their all night struggle, God touched the socket of Jacob's hip and damaged it. Thereafter Jacob limped, a constant reminder of his fateful encounter with God.

At this time Jacob also received a new name, Israel, which probably means, "God rules." His name change was significant because the old name "Jacob" means "supplanter." Jacob moved into a new phase in his life in which he was blessed yet led with permanent limp. He was now fit to lead.

Testing of leaders is one of the most vital tests of their preparation. By that I do not believe that untested leaders can't have good character and be well disciplined in their understanding of Christian truth and be truly effective. I do believe, though, a remarkable quality comes from the lives of leaders after they have wrestled with God and life. And the resulting limp is a reminder to themselves and a sign to others that God has humbled them. "Blessed is the man who perseveres under trial," James says, "because when he has stood the test, he will receive the crown of life that God has promised to those who love him" [James 1:12- see also 1 Corinthians 9:25; 2 Timothy 4:8].

Peter is an excellent illustration of a leader that walked with a limp.

Toward the end of Jesus' public ministry, the Lord concentrated on preparing the disciples for His coming suffering and death. When Peter first heard of this, he took Jesus aside and rebuked Him. "Never Lord!" he said. "This shall not happen to you!" [Matthew 16:22]. But Jesus was not pleased with Peter. He said, "Get behind me Satan! You do not have in mind the things of God, but rather the things of men" [Matthew 16:23].

Why did Jesus rebuke Peter so harshly? Peter couldn't comprehend Jesus' words, for his idea of what a Messiah should be and do had no room for a Roman cross. And I believe Peter didn't quite understand the significance of Jesus' rebuke until after the resurrection.

Shortly after the Last Supper, Jesus and Peter had a similar exchange. Jesus prophesied that He would be taken away that

> I do believe, though, a remarkable quality comes from the lives of leaders after they have wrestled with God and life. And the resulting limp is a reminder to themselves and a sign to others that God has humbled them.

night by the religious authorities and Roman soldiers and that all the disciples would fall away. Peter protested, "Even if all fall away on account of you, I never will" [Matthew 26:33]. Jesus said to Peter that that "very night, before the rooster crows, you will disown me three times" [Matthew 26:34]. However, Peter [along with the other disciples] said, "I will never disown you" [verse 35].

That evening in the garden, Peter drew his sword and cut off the ear of a servant of the high priest who had come to arrest Jesus. I am confident that at that moment Peter would have gladly died to protect the Lord. Yet, only a few minutes later he turned on Jesus. How did his zeal change to cowardliness so quickly?

I believe that up to the arrest, Peter thought Jesus was going to march triumphantly into Jerusalem and establish Himself as King, run out the Herodians, turn back the Romans and reestablish the line of David. Peter probably envisioned himself as holding a prominent position in

Jesus' reign. Whenever Jesus spoke of His arrest and crucifixion, Peter became agitated and lost his sense of direction and identity. Roman arrest and crucifixion didn't fit with the kingly reign Peter had in mind for Jesus.

So, when Jesus was arrested, Peter's world crashed in around him. He was so dismayed by the arrest that when a servant girl asked him if he was a disciple, Peter said, "I don't know what you're talking about" [Matthew 26:70]. After two more denials, the rooster crowed, and "the Lord turned and looked straight at Peter." Of course Peter remembered Jesus' prophecy; he went outside and wept bitterly.

Peter's failure to maintain faith under fire reveals several important truths for untested Christian leaders. First, we must understand that the true test of Peter's identity with the Lord Jesus Christ came at the point of relationship and identification with the true Christ.

When Peter denied Jesus, it wasn't primarily over a doctrinal issue. Nor did he yield to sexual immorality. Peter's failure was more fundamental: he was disloyal to the Lord Himself. Peter lost heart and trust when Jesus failed to fulfill his expectations of what a Messiah should be.

Peter had expected a Messiah of his own making. He had assumed the Lord was coming to establish an earthly kingdom, so when Jesus yielded Himself to His enemies, Peter was demoralized and lost all sense of identity and value. He failed to see the difference between a temporal and eternal King.

All too often in my counseling with young pastors I have found that they become so wrapped up in their quest for success, advancement and visibility that they have little understanding how to serve God in a hidden, humble way. Like Peter, they serve a God of their own making— the triumphant god of Success, not the Suffering Servant of the Cross. They don't understand that at its most fundamental point, ministry involves faithfulness and humility of heart and mind.

The second lesson to learn from Peter is that, in spite of failure, restoration is possible; but it will be restoration with a limp. After testing, we never again have confidence in our own insights, opinions and abilities. Our self-confidence is replaced by humility, a sense of being under God's grace and dependent on His Word.

After the resurrection, Jesus appeared before the disciples and three times asked Peter, "Do you truly love me?" The first two times Jesus used the Greek word for love, agape, meaning a love in which our entire personality, including the will is involved. Peter answered, "Yes, Lord, you know that I love you." Peter used a different Greek word—phileo—for love, meaning a spontaneous natural affection or fondness in which emotion plays a more prominent role than will. Peter couldn't say with confidence that he loved Jesus with agape love, for he was painfully aware that he had denied Him.

When Jesus asked Peter a third time if he loved Him, he substituted phileo for agape, and in so doing, communicated to Peter on a level that he could respond. Jesus knew that Peter's confession was based on the realizations of personal failure and inability to love God fully in his own strength. The underlying idea was that Peter knew that he was a failure without Jesus. All Peter could promise was a limited human love of Jesus.

After each of Peter's three responses, Jesus reminds them of the mission they are called to. Then the Lord commanded, "feed my lambs." Jesus was being generous and kind, affirming Peter three times so as to forgive his three denials and restore him to ministry. From that point forward, Peter only had confidence in God's grace [John 21:15-19].

The third lesson to be learned from Peter's trial is that when testing comes, our character and destiny are revealed. Each of the twelve was tested. Judas, the son of perdition, went on to an eternity separated from God. The remaining eleven, while tested severely and failing at many points, came through and were restored. And they had a new quality of reverence for and dependence on Jesus.

All children of God go through testing; that's a promise [Hebrews 12:1-13]. However, if we don't anticipate and expect it, we'll be surprised and confused when it comes; our limp will be an occasion for bitterness rather than a reminder of God's presence and Lordship.

Scripture also refers to our trials as siftings, instances in which God allows Satan to test our faith, as he did with Job. Approaching God and claiming that Job is righteous only because he is blessed, Satan says, "But stretch out your hand and strike everything he has, and he will surely curse you to your face" [Job 1:11]. Remarkably, God grants permission to Satan to sift Job; the remainder of the book is the story of how Job responded to his trial.

One of the most important lessons we learn from Job is that sifting is a part of the purging process that God uses for cleansing and reorienting our priorities. "In this you greatly rejoice," Peter wrote, "though now for a little while you may have had to suffer grief in all kinds of trials. These have come so that your faith—of greater worth than gold, which perishes even though refined by fire—may be proved genuine and may result in praise, glory, and honor when Jesus Christ is revealed [1 Peter 1:6-7].

If anything characterizes seasoned leaders, it is enduring qualities like humility and faithfulness, characteristics that make them look like Jesus. So, pastors that walk with a limp usually run the best race. They may not be the swiftest, but they know what they have been called into. And they are rarely disqualified for taking shortcuts. In the end, they are the ones holding the gold.

BLESSED ARE THE FLEXIBLE

Flexibility is another important characteristic of good leaders. For years, Moses had led Israel in the wilderness by judging all the civil cases himself. This had possibly grown without Moses rethinking alternatives until the people stood around Moses from the morning until the evening. Jethro, Moses' father-in-law, saw the problem, proposed a solution and Moses trained and delegated, helping both the leader and the people [Exodus 18:13-26].

Jesus deliberately violated the manmade rules of the Sabbath, F.F. Bruce believes, in order to keep the disciples flexible and willing to make change. "The Sabbath was made for the man and not man for the Sabbath," He said [Mark 2:23-28].

Paul's time-proven strategy for church planting was to go to major cities in un-evangelized areas and to preach in the synagogue. On Paul's second missionary journey, Paul and his team were attempting to work this plan by going into Asia and then next into Bithynia, but the Holy

Spirit would not permit them [Acts 16:6-8].

At the same time, consider what James is addressing in chapter 3. James isn't criticizing the planning process necessarily, but he is encouraging us to keep listening and obeying the Lord saying, "If the Lord wills, we shall live and also do this or that."

Or said another way, we should always ask, "What is the Father doing?" If Jesus could only do what the Father was revealing to Him, then what about you and me? Our model for being flexible is Jesus! (John 5:19).

Conclusion

AN INTERVIEW WITH JOHN

Following are excerpts from an interview John did with Bridgebuilder (1988) concerning his perspective on evangelism and about how God uses him in praying for the sick, and he offers some advice to those in ministry.

BB: "There is a distinct difference between the conservative evangelical mind in approaching evangelism and the charismatic mind. The conservatives will say, 'Well Jesus taught that he was a teacher.' The charismatics, of course, want fire to fall. They want evangelism through signs and wonders. John, do you feel there is a balance between these two approaches—or is only one of them the biblical mode of evangelism?"

John: "Those who identify with conservative evangelicals would be governed by certain philosophical precepts that sound something like this: 'God exists. God is logical. Therefore a God program, presentation and ministry must be communicated in the most logical, sensible way that our minds, coupled with an earnest desire for the Holy Spirit's unction, can produce.' And so the underlying idea is that men must be convinced to receive Christ. At the same time, I don't know a single conservative evangelical who wouldn't embrace the notion—as it's communicated in John 3—that all men must be born from on high, a combination of a man calling upon, turning to and believing in Christ. The perception is that man's faith in God, who has provoked it in the first place, produces a new creation in Christ Jesus. On that much Pentecostals, charismatics, third-wave and conservative evangelicals would agree.

"Now Pentecostals and charismatics have also embraced the idea that there's a second work scenario that both follows and adds to the born again experience. At the same time, many evangelicals and third-wave people would propose that after that, there are a number of subsequent fillings of the Spirit that could have many different benefits for the believer. Pentecostals and charismatics would agree with that also. So there are points on which we diverge and points on which we come together.

"Now, to speak directly to your question: When it comes to evangelism, there is a difference in the mindset of those who mostly adhere to what I would call Western rationalism. In the western world, we have accepted pure rationalism as a consequence of the Enlightment. Progressively our worldview becomes more scientific and more natura-listic. As a result, most of us read the Bible with sort of 'rationalistic world-lenses' that screen out supernatural events and organize them to naturalistic explanations; therefore most conservative evangelicals that I know have perspectives in terms of what they anticipate God to do. For instance, one conservative camp can't conceive of God working outside of Scripture other than the means by which you know God. Whereas a broader type of evangelical Christianity would say that God is able to communicate with His children outside of Scripture, but subordinate to the Word."

BB: "How do you go about speaking, as you do, to Christians who do not accept the supernatural? How do you minister gifts of healing to them when they do not believe that healing happens for today?"

"I'm not always successful with every audience, or with every portion of every audience. But there is an ever-increasing number of people with whom I have had some success, and there are a significant number of writers, thinkers, theologians and pastors all over the world who are con-tributing to an ever-growing body of literature and thought that's addressing this issue."

"I think that one of the basic problems is that most people have never had a course on worldview. Your momma didn't set you at her knee and say, 'Honey, now this is our worldview. This is what we allow as truth, and this is what we say is fantasy and not based on fact.' But in reality, you were conditioned, from childhood forward, by teachers and others in your life to discount one thing and accept another. So you have been conditioned into a worldview. Just saying that to an audience makes them aware that it exists and starts them in a process of deciding: 'to what degree does my conditioning control my scriptural understand-ing?'"

BB: "So you purposely talk to them about their worldview?"

John: "Yes. Now I'd like to return to your first question about intellectual evangelism versus power evangelism. The conservative evangelical is presupposing a presence and an anointing of the Holy Spirit. He is committed to the idea that he needs to make as logical and passionate a presentation of the Gospel as he can. The difference is that the average Pentecostal or charismatic is looking for leading from the Holy Spirit that the conservative person isn't allowing for.

For instance, when we train people in power evangelism, we would say that the opportunity to pray for the sick can be a major boon and blessing and foundation for presenting the Gospel. I can point out a number of texts where that happens in the New Testament."

"Furthermore, we point out the reality of the opportunity to cast out demons may present itself as a foundation for presenting the Gospel. And again, we show places in the New Testament where that happened."

"Third, raising the dead may be an opportunity for presenting the Gospel. Well those three categories are out of the question for most conservative evangelicals."

"Let's take something more natural—just the selection of the target audience. The charismatic/Pentecostal/third-wave person may be walking through the streets or marketplace praying, 'Lord, show me who the Holy Spirit is on. Who's ready?' This is operating on the presuppositions that God is in the world, He's drawing men and women unto Himself by the Spirit and that we can discern that activity."

"The conservative evangelical would take the first two steps and ignore the third. They do not think they can discern—although they'll all tell stories about occasions where that exact thing happens. But they see that as the exception rather than the rule. They would agree with charismatics who say that the providence of God produced that experience, but they don't think it can happen regularly. They would argue vehemently that you can't anticipate this as normal providence of God."

"But I disagree. I believe that you can anticipate it, and that's what characterized the New Testament evangelism experience. I believe supernatural intervention can characterize our experience today."

BB: "There is a trend among charismatics. Many are saying, 'I see a lot of the talk gifts. Every Sunday, we hear almost the same prophecies from the same people. But why is it we're not seeing the power gifts?' Would you talk to that?"

John: "I think we're dealing with three factors. One factor is this: Pentecostalism began largely on a poverty, lower-class level, although there were certainly well-educated, sophisticated people involved. Each ensuing generation has gotten better educated and better established in society. The second factor is the process toward legitimization and acceptance. What I'm saying is that you can be educated out of Pentecost. I've met dozens of pastors in mainline churches—Presbyterian, Methodist, and so on—and some of these people are teaching in major seminaries, whose grandparents were involved in founding Pentecostalism. But they couldn't stay in Pentecostalism because they got educated—they grew progressively more embarrassed about their roots and more sensitized through the educational process to what was going on in the context of Pentecostal history."

"There is a third factor. Now, I'm speaking as an outsider looking in. I want Pentecostal and charismatic readers to excuse me because I'm ignorant on some points, and I may say something that is inaccurate, but it's my observation. Across the board, within the context of fundamentalism today—whether it's Pentecostal, charismatic or not—there's been a progression towards theatre. For instance, if you watch any evangelical telecast, there's theatre involved. There's music, drama, pathos…theatre. The presentation, the message itself has theatrical overtones."

"Now, theatre presumes the ability to control audience interest. Therefore, it eliminates the exercise of the unknown, taking of chances, reaching out for something you're not sure of, listening for the nuance of the Spirit's breathing and speaking to you."

"People tend to prophecy similar if not the same prophecies over and over again. Why? Well, it's become safe. As long as we do it with the proper theatre—the right pitch, the right tone, the right 'King James-isms' we've done something that's acceptable."

"Preaching has the same assumptions. Deliverance has the same assumptions. They're controlled much the same way."

"Therefore, the conscious awareness of the need to make this 'come off' has eliminated much of the naïve, childlike practice of early Pentecost in which there was no thought of an audience but God. People were just interacting with their God. God said, 'Do this!' And they got up and did it."

"Now we've got cameras on, and we've got audio running, and we've got to get that money in to pay for that building and that overhead. We can't take time to just interact with our God. Over a period of time, this has developed insensitivity on the part of the whole group because they all know they're being manipulated. The pastor is being manipulated, the choir is being manipulated and the church is being manipulated."

"Manipulated by what? By the need to produce a good experience for everybody. The goal has become theatre and good experience, over against interaction between God and His people, His word and His Spirit. All of that is still there in the shadow, but not in substance. The language, the nomenclature, the focus is still there."

"How do we back out of this situation? By making our service dull? No. I think we have to find an acceptable way to instill reality again, to instill sanity again. I think everybody is a little tired of this. Let's get on our faces and call out to God and let Him deal with us afresh. Let's lay down the theatre for awhile."

"Now, I don't want to equate theatre with pretense because I think there's a lot more honesty and a lot more sincerity and even integrity than pretense would allow for. I don't think anyone has intentionally promoted or orchestrated this shift. I think it has evolved."

BB: "In a real sense, you're not talking about pretense. You're talking about a shift of focus. We've said, 'Something good happened one time, and it happened when we did this. So let's repeat this and try to repeat the success.'"

John: "Exactly."

BB: "Let's say I'm a pastor of what seems to be a big, on fire, charismatic church. We've got the big choir, an orchestra to accompany our worship, and everything is great. All of a sudden, I wake up one morning with this horrendous pounding voice in the back of my head that says, 'This is dead as a stick.' What do I do?"

John: (Long pause) "Well, I'm afraid all too often you just keep going right on going because you've got this payroll, these people who depend on you, this background of support people that you can't let down and mentors whom you have to respond to. You become progressively more dishonest all the time, and you live the kind of life where you become empty. I'm afraid that's where many people are at today."

"In part, it's because of the American dream—rags to riches, be a success at any cost. There's some sort of amalgamation of worldly ambition versus a sincere desire to do what God wants. We equate the advance of the institution with the growth of the Church i.e. the Body of Christ."

"I once had to face up to the fact that, as a successful pastor, I was living this kind of life. I had just read the riot act to a young man. I'd said, 'I'll see you Sunday morning in church.' I turned around and walked out of the building when God spoke to me. He said, 'Would you come to this church next Sunday if you weren't paid to?' I realized the answer to that was 'No.' I had long since stopped enjoying it."

So I stumbled into my office and prayed and asked God the fatal question, 'God, what's wrong with me?' He began showing me. He showed me that through a process of time I quenched the Spirit again and again and again as I chose allegiance to organization and institutions over against following Him. Now, institution is to wagon as organism is to horse. You do fine if the wagon is hitched behind the horse. But when you put the wagon before the horse, you're in trouble. In my case, I put the horse under the wagon. The institution was killing me."

"I repented of that. I resigned my position and probably would have never gone back into the pastorate again—except the Lord called me to it and told me it wouldn't be that day this time. And it hasn't been. But I'm ready at any time to abandon all of it if it gets to a place where I am serving the institution again rather than serving God."

BB: "If I were a pastor who found myself in that dry, dead place you described, how would you counsel me?"

John: "I would encourage you to recoup integrity and honesty first by sincerely going before God in prayer and fasting. Sequester yourself away for a few weeks and ask God for specific direction. You got to that place by making decisions, and you get out of it by making decisions. What you need is God's guidance."

"It might be that the second thing is to go before the people and say, 'You know, we've gotten here, and I'm not exactly sure how. But I, for one, am not all that excited about it. And I would like to turn around now and see if we can find our way back to a place where yea is yea and nay is nay, and we all know it. I will quit manipulating you if you quit manipulating me, and the institution will quit manipulating both of us. Let's have real integrity before one another and God.' I think the characteristics of such a move would be confession of sin, confession of faults and an open lifestyle—self disclosure and a willingness to be a part of a body that examines, loves and nurtures one another."

BB: "Why, in your opinion, do we see so few ministries that are built on the demonstration of signs and wonders?"

John: "I think we're dealing with several problems. One problem is that pastors who believe in the potential of the miraculous have tended to believe that only certain individuals are anointed for this kind of ministry. There's certainly biblical precedent for that. If you look at the Bible, Old and New Testaments, signs and wonders occur under certain leadership during certain periods of time up until the Gospels. But that could even be taken as a section of time or period of history. So we think of the anointed one, the one whom God has blessed specifically. That's been an underlying presupposition of Pentecostalism from the outset."

"A second and contrasting view is the oft-quoted statement—and I've read a lot of Pentecostal literature—that this generation, this movement, this group is going to move God's power from the pulpit to the pews, that we're going to release power to the people—yet that never seems to happen."

"A third factor is that anyone who is anointed by God is, by virtue of that, no longer able to remain a layman. He must now become a pastor. A Catholic kid, if he loves Jesus at all, has got to become a priest. Well, in the Pentecostal church, he's got to become a pastor or evangelist."

"There's no role for the layman who's gifted. He ends up a deacon, a servant. He drives cars, ushers people around, teaches Sunday school and sings in the choir. But to be moving in power as a layman—there's no place for that, no role for it."

"Last of all, the Church tends to inspire and educate, but doesn't equip, and we need all three [see Ephesians 4:11]. Only recently have we seen the training of layman as an authentic and important responsibility. Within Pentecostal framework we've seen the rise of the discipleship movement. Today, some of us are saying, 'there's more yet,' and it's called equipping the saints unto ministry. That means in the roles of apostle, prophet, evangelist, pastor and teacher."

"I don't know how many have gone through our training as to date, but I know that we've had nearly a half a million people in our training sessions in the last six or seven years. I would guess 50 percent of the ones that came are still discipling and multiplying other disciples. There might be 700,000-800,000 people now that are praying for the sick, casting out demons and winning the lost. I think in another fifteen years or so there will be several million worldwide who are able to do this stuff. Could you imagine 100,000 people in Washington D.C. who could cast out demons, heal the sick and win the lost under supernatural unction? What would that do in the society?"

BB: "Can you describe to me what it feels like when you're ministering and you sense the presence of the Holy Spirit—or you sense that this is the time for healing to happen? What do you feel?"

John: "Sometimes nothing, and sometimes everything. I operate basically on a disclosure of Scripture. I have to be obedient to the call of God. God has told me to heal the sick. Therefore, if somebody walks up to me and says, 'I'm sick, will you pray for me?' I feel that my duty is to pray for them."

"I also feel it's important that I tell them where I am at the moment. I may not be in the most spiritual condition. So I want them to know, 'This is probably not your best shot. But I'm willing, out of obedience, to do it.' A lot of times people get healed anyways."

"Whenever healing occurs, there are at least three dimensions at work. Sometimes it's the faith of the healer, meaning that God is healing through me. Sometimes it's because of the faith of the person being healed. And sometimes a friend has prompted the whole thing by faith."

"I remember standing at a urinal in an airport in Phoenix. A guy leaned over and put his face in front of mine and said, 'You're him, aren't you?' He wanted to shake hands with me. I said, 'I'm a little busy right now.' He said, 'Will you pray for me?' I said, 'Before or after I wash my hands?' This actually happened! I couldn't believe it!"

"So I washed my hands and prayed for him."

"I heard through a friend of his that he was healed. I think he was prompted by limited social skills on one hand and desperation to get healed on the other. Maybe the Holy Spirit even prompted him. Somebody had faith. Right at that moment all I had was anger. I never felt so put upon in my life! It certainly wasn't my faith, but I did do what Jesus commissioned me to do. I went through the motions of it."

"On the other end of the continuum there are times of great anointing and presence that can have physiological as well as spiritual and emotional impact on me. There are times when my whole body feels in the grips of something—power, energy. My legs and knees shake. My upper torso feels energized. There's literally something like electricity coming out of my hands when I'm touching people. Sometimes bolts of energy just explode out of my hands. That's usually when miraculous kinds of things take place. It happens once in a thousand times. But it happens two or three times a year, and I never know when it's going to start happening."

"But on the continuum from feeling nothing to feeling everything, I spend most of the time down in this quadrant here [toward the nothing side] just out of sincere desire to obey God doing what I do. It's like saying your prayers before you go to bed or grace over your food, or getting up and trying to get your body reasonably clean so you can maintain relationships with people. You just do these kinds of things because it's the right thing to do."

"You see, nearly anybody can put his hand on somebody and say, 'Lord, I don't know exactly how to pray, but please bless this person. Heal him and touch his body.' That's all I'm trying to get people to do. I think God will reward it powerfully."

Appendix A

PRAYING IN THE SPIRIT

T The first thing to do about the area of praying in the Spirit is to define the term. For a working definition I would say that speaking in tongues is Spirit-inspired speaking in which the conscious mind plays no part. It is the speaking of a language (whether known or angelic) which is unlearned by the speaker.

The book of 1 Corinthians gives us some idea of the purpose of tongues: (1) They are a means of supernatural, inspired communication to God (1 Corinthians 14); (2) They edify the speaker even if others are not edified (14:4); (3) They do bring edification to the Body when properly interpreted. Tongues + Interpretation = Prophecy in edification value (14:5); (4) They can serve as a sign to the unbeliever (14:22).

Here Paul uses a first century hermeneutic to say that tongues "improperly used" (i.e., without interpretation) can be viewed as a judgment to an unbeliever who would leave the meeting never to return because of his belief that everyone was mad (v.23). This, in the final analysis, could be damnation to the unbeliever's spirit.(5) They can be used in private to pray and sing to God. In this case no interpretation is needed because no one is there to hear (14:14-15).

It is clear from 1 Corinthians 14:15 that Paul recognizes a kind of charismatic hymnody, both a singing in tongues (with the Spirit) and with intelligible words (with the mind). This was probably a spontaneous type of singing. The same is likely to be true of 14:26, which speaks of public use of tongues. In the parallel passages of Ephesians 5:19 and Colossians 3:16, Paul mentions three forms of singing: psalms, hymns and spiritual songs. It appears that Paul also has in mind here charismatic singing. This is the practice in public worship, which is usually called singing in the Spirit.

Two factors point to this conclusion:

First, in this context, Paul is speaking about being continually filled with the Spirit. He is urging the spontaneity, which comes from the impulse of the Holy Spirit as contrasted with that which comes from the stimulus of wine.

Second, the word "spiritual" used in both passages characterizes the song as one which is prompted by the Spirit. It is not clear that Paul intends three different distinct kinds of music. The adjective "spiritual" probably embraces all three nouns. On the other hand, even if "spiritual" belongs solely to songs, the distinction between the first two (psalms and hymns) and the third (spiritual songs) would not be between established liturgical forms of spontaneous singing of intelligible words and spontaneous singing in tongues.

1 Corinthians 14:14-15: "For if I pray in a tongue, my spirit prays, but my mind is unfruitful. So what shall I do? I will pray with my spirit, but I will also pray with my mind; I will sing with my spirit, but I will also sing with my mind."

In Jude 20 and Ephesians 6:18, we are exhorted by the authors to pray in the Spirit. The phrase "in the Spirit" in early Christian literature usually carried the meaning of being under the control of the Spirit or under the inspiration of the Spirit. Here the phrase is connected with praying.

The indication is that the word "pray" used here had become a technical way to indicate the Charismatic prayer in which the words are given by the Spirit. Praying in the Spirit includes then, but is not restricted to, prayer in tongues. I believe that Charismatic prayer, including glossolalic prayer, can be presumed for both Jude 20 and Ephesians 6:18.

WHO CAN PRAY IN THE SPIRIT?

One of the most often asked a question is, "Are tongues for everyone?" So far in my experience, it has been. I have not seen anyone yet who wanted to speak in tongues that has not received it, although I have seen some who struggle with it.

Most who have problems come from a background which as an anti-tongues theology. They have been taught that this is not a present-day gift to experience. Unlearning for these people often takes time. Scriptural opposition is usually raised from the passage in 1 Corinthians, which asks the question, "Do all speak in tongues?" It is often pointed out that the Greek language requires a "no" as the answer.

On the surface this seems an adequate response; however the context of the whole passage must be taken into consideration. The context begins with 1 Corinthians 11:17 and continues through 14:40. Without taking you through all the reasons, let me suggest that I think the key is when the body comes together. Within that frame of reference, Paul is asking the questions recorded at the end of the chapter 12. When the Body comes together, "Are all Apostles?" "No!" "Do all have the gifts of healing?" "No!" "Do all speak in tongues?" "No!" "Do all interpret?" "No!"

This passage does not mean that all cannot speak in tongues. It does mean that when the Body of Christ gets together, all do not have to speak in tongues.

There are five reasons why I believe one ought to pray in the Spirit.

1) It can be a sign for unbelievers (1 Corinthians 14:22).

2) It is a form of petition (Ephesians 6:18).

3) It can be a time of edification for the one praying (1 Corinthians 14:4).

4) It is a part of our spiritual armament (Ephesians 6:18).

5) It gives praise to God (1 Corinthians 14:2).

Appendix B

RESTORING FALLEN LEADERS

Over the past several years the Church has been rocked time and again by revelations of sexual and financial misconduct among some of its best-known leaders. But just as alarming for me are daily reports of failed local pastors, men and women who may not garner headlines but whose sin has direct impact in the lives of rank and file Christians.

Besides the obvious embarrassment and shame that come with exposure of seedy acts, fallen leaders betray their followers' trust, damaging a God-ordained bond between pastor and congregation. And especially damaging is the disrepute brought on the pastoral calling itself. Faithful pastors have found it more difficult to lead in the past several years. Through no fault of their own, the office has been tarnished.

Under these circumstances, we shouldn't be too surprised that many Christians are confused, hurt and even cynical about leadership. But the problem isn't merely emotional; Christians are divided over how to treat fallen leaders.

What about restoration? The treatment of those that have fallen is based on God's treatment of all sinners: the cross. At the cross forgiveness and reconciliation are extended to all who trust in Christ. Implicit to the work of the cross is restoration of the fallen, the establishment of fruitful lives and ministries in God's Kingdom. Leaders are no different.

The Bible contains several examples of fallen leaders who were restored. In the Old Testament, David was restored after he abused his power and position by having an affair with Bathsheba and murdering her husband. Moses returned to lead Israel out of Egypt after committing murder and running away. In the New Testament, Peter was restored after he denied Christ three times.

There is no question in my mind that fallen leaders can be restored. But saying restoration is possible raises a more difficult and complex question: what qualifications must they meet before they can be restored?

When leaders fall, we have a responsibility to love, forgive and receive them back into the Body of Christ, as we would any repentant sinner.

But does genuinely forgiving their sin mean they should remain our leaders? If we fail to return leaders to office, does that mean we don't love them, that in fact we hold their sin against them? In other words, does immediate restoration to ministry automatically accompany forgiveness? I think not.

If the individual sin itself were the only obstacle to leadership, restoration would be tied exclusively to receiving forgiveness. But far too often individual sins reflect the more troublesome problem of a flawed character. For this reason, repentance and forgiveness are prerequisites for entering the restoration process, not qualifications for completing the process.

The Bible requires fallen leaders to step down from ministry at least temporarily because they no longer meet the moral qualifications of an overseer, qualifications that are much higher for leaders than for other Christians. They are no longer "above reproach...temperate, self-controlled, respectable... [Having] a good reputation with outsiders..." [1 Timothy 3:1-7].

PUNISHMENT?

An inability to understand or accept the unique character of Christian leadership leads to erroneous conclusions about restoration. Recently I read an article in which the author argued that, like a corrupt businessman who serves his prison sentence, once a fallen pastor has been "punished," he should be given a "second chance." The author illustrates his point by describing how quickly a former executive was hired after serving prison time for illegal securities trading. The writer even goes so far as to say fallen leaders may be better leaders than those who haven't tasted serious sin! He asks, "Does the secular world understand forgiveness better than we do?" I think not. The author confuses restoration with punishment. He fails to recognize that the restoration of a leader involves the rebuilding of his character, not the successful completion of a penal sentence.

Christian leaders are different from the world's leaders. For example, many doctors do not follow their own advice. But we don't expect doctors to personify health. We go to them for expert advice and knowledge about medicine. But pastors who fail to embody the moral and spiritual values that they preach undermine their message of personal transformation through Christ. Paul could say, "Follow my example," because he followed "the example of Christ" [1 Corinthians 11:1]. Christian leaders' expertise and advice are only as genuine as the quality of their character.

Fallen leaders also must recognize that they are not the only ones in need of healing and renewal: the people they lead have also been hurt. The leaders have violated a sacred trust, and trust is the very foundation of their leadership. Trust—the firm belief in the honesty and reliability of another—is a most fragile quality; it takes years to build, but only minutes to destroy. Once destroyed, trust may take years to rebuild again.

Fallen leaders must overcome many obstacles before they are restored, which complicates our relationship with them while they are working through the consequences of sin. So, to know how to treat a fallen leader we must know the path to restoration, for we will walk it with them. The following guidelines capture the main elements of restoration. I introduce each guideline as a question. If you are unsure how to relate to a fallen leader who is on the road to restoration, ask these questions about them; your answers will help clarify how God wants you to treat them.

[1] Does the leader exhibit the fruits of true repentance?

Scripture offers clear, concrete guidelines from which we can discern true repentance. The Greek word translated as "repentance" in English versions of the New Testament is *metanoia*, which means literally, "changing one's mind." The first step of changing one's mind about sin is admitting we have done something wrong.

Admitting sin isn't merely feeling bad about being found out; it's deep remorse over sin. This involves true confession, acknowledging sin to all who have been sinned against and who may be hurt by it. Of course, true confession starts with God. Does the fallen leader willing divulge all sins, or does he/she appear to only to tell those things they have been caught doing? In other words, is he/she hiding anything?

In Psalm 32, David describes the relationship between confession and forgiveness. "When I kept silent, my bones wasted away through my groaning all day long. For day and night your hand was heavy upon me; my strength was sapped as in the heat of summer. Then I acknowledged my sin to you and did not cover up my iniquity. I said, 'I will confess my transgressions to the Lord'—and you forgave the guilt of my sin."

David couldn't go on hiding his sin, for left unconfessed it was becoming a spiritual cancer. As David demonstrates, confession must also be to his congregation. First Timothy 5:20 says that elders are to be "rebuked publicly." What exactly does Paul mean by a public rebuke? To rebuke is to reprimand, to scold in a sharp way; the fallen elder is told to stop his sinning...immediately. Paul also says the rebuke is to take place among people against whom the fallen leader sinned; elders have a public ministry, so they are to be corrected in public. Implicit to a public rebuke is the fallen leader's confession of grief over his sin.

This passage isn't saying a leader owes a detailed confession to the congregation, though it does raise questions about how much detail a fallen leader should reveal. Many Christians think it is inappropriate to require fallen leaders to confess their sins explicitly before their congregations, that somehow this invades their "right to privacy." But leaders forfeit their right to privacy when they accept God's call; their lives are supposed to be examples of what they teach, living testaments of God's grace. Part of being an example is coming clean with sin.

For example, Paul rebuked Peter and Barnabas publicly [Galatians 2:11-14]. And what about Nathan and David in the Old Testament [2 Samuel 12]? We know everything about these leaders, the good and the bad. God isn't as concerned about protecting fallen leaders' reputations as either we or they are.

Confession to fellow elders must be specific and complete; they need to know details so they can determine how to approach restitution and restoration. But the congregation doesn't need explicit detail, though the confession must clearly acknowledge the nature of the sin. If the fallen leader is vague about his/her sin, misunderstanding and gossip may follow him the rest of his/her life.

True repentance is motivated by brokenness of heart and the desire to protect God's people—not the desire to retain position and power or to cover up sin. After the prophet Nathan confronted David for his abuse of power and privilege, David said, "The sacrifices of God are a broken spirit; a broken and contrite heart O God, you will not despise. In your good pleasure make Zion prosper; build up the walls of Jerusalem" [Psalm 51:17-18].

David's concern was for Israel's glory, not his position as king. His repentance was true.

The second mark of repentance is a firm and spoken renunciation of the sin. Proverbs 28:13 says, "He who conceals his sin does not prosper, but whoever confesses and renounces them finds mercy." Renunciation means a willingness to do anything to stop sinning.

This is what Jesus had in mind in Matthew 18:8-9 when he told the disciples to cut off their hand or pluck out their eye if either caused them to stumble. He wasn't telling them to literally cut off a limb or poke out an eye; he was saying that no action was too extreme in avoiding sin.

The third mark of repentance is reconciliation. In Matthew 5:23-25, Jesus instructs us to seek reconciliation with someone we have wronged before worshipping God. Reconciliation involves taking responsibility for our sin, confessing to the person we have wronged and asking for his or her forgiveness. For the spouses of leaders guilty of sexual wrongdoing, reconciliation is usually a complex and long-term process. It is also the most critical step of repentance, one that requires much of the leader's energy and attention.

An important part of reconciliation is a willingness to make restitution for harm done to others. Zacchaeus, the corrupt tax collector [most tax collectors were corrupt in those days], responded to Jesus' call by offering to make restitution: "Look Lord! Here and now I give half of my possessions to the poor, and if I have cheated anybody out of anything, I will pay back four times the amount" [Luke 19:8]. Zacchaeus's act of restitution embodied faith in God; Jesus pronounced him saved that very moment.

Restitution frequently involves more than money. For example, a leader guilty of sexual wrongdoing owes restitution to his congregation or organization; he must fix broken trust though his/her open repentance and a humble willingness to do whatever necessary to repair the harm. How is this done? In the very least, by patiently understanding that the people need time to heal from broken trust.

Sometimes the organization may owe restitution for sin committed by the fallen leader when he/she acted on its behalf.

For example, the leader may have had extramarital affairs with women from other churches or he/she may have misused others' funds. The organization will need to ask for forgiveness, rebuild broken bridges and, in some instances, pay financial restitution.

Fallen pastors who truly repent are broken by the experience. Their public lives become transparent; they are no longer willing to live a lie around other Christians. When it comes time to confess their sins to the congregations, there is no sense of their covering up anything. They recognize that they betrayed a trust and brought scandal on the people of God, and they are willing to release their ministerial influence over the people. They no longer find their identity in their pastoral position; they are now truly broken before God.

[2] Is the leader's sin the result of a momentary moral lapse or part of habitual, cunning and deceptive sin that reflects a seriously flawed character?

There is a significant difference between the consequences of momentary sin that comes from a one time temptation and sin that is prolonged and flagrant. An isolated act of passion must be dealt with differently from long-time, premeditated sin. The former, though serious, may be repented of and dealt with quickly; the latter represents a seriously flawed, immature character that could take years to reclaim.

I once knew a pastor named Bill [not his real name] who had a difficult marriage. His wife was like Gomer, the unfaithful wife of the prophet Hosea in the Old Testament. Yet Bill remained faithful to his wife despite her flirtatious manners.

Bill suffered periodic bouts with depression and loneliness. One day, when in the midst of one of Bill's emotionally difficult times, he gave in to temptation and had sex with a woman he had been counseling. The minute she left his office he phoned one of the elders and confessed everything to him. The elders called a meeting that evening, and Bill repeated his story, then turned in his resignation. He also asked if he could confess his sin to the entire congregation.

Bill's elders wisely refused to accept his resignation, instead placing him on a leave of absence. He was allowed to confess to the church and ask for forgiveness. The elders determined Bill's problem was not part of a long history of sin or the result of a serious character flaw. Rather, it was a one-time failing, under stressful circumstances, of a good man.

The elders recommended that Bill receive time off for counseling to work through his troubled marriage and moral failure. Six months later Bill returned as pastor, and he has faithfully served the congregation ever since. The church was able to accept Bill back immediately because they understood the circumstances surrounding his sin, felt his brokenness and sensed he wasn't hiding anything from them.

SECRET SIN

Fallen leaders with a long history of serious sin face a far more difficult and longer road to restoration than Bill. They must overcome habit patterns of cunning, deception and secret sin built up through the years of disobedience—sin that they are unwilling or able to control.

The length and complexity of the restoration process is tied directly to the length and nature of the sin. Commenting on this, John White and Ken Blue, in their book, Healing the Wounded, write:

"People who abuse power are changed progressively as they do so. In abusing power they give themselves over to evil, untruth, self-blindedness, and hardness without allowing themselves or anyone else to see what is happening. The longer the process continues, the harder repentance comes."

Because of this, nipping sin in the bud is especially important for the restoration of leaders. Many fallen leaders with a long history of secret sin never make it back into the ministry. When they truly repent, the severity and effects of their sin are so great that they have forfeited the privilege of leadership. If they do make it back into leadership, the process takes many difficult years.

[3] Is the leader accountable to others as he works through the restoration process?

There is no recovery process for a leader with a hardened heart, but there are many paths back for the truly repentant. Most people aren't close enough to their pastors to discern the difference between true and false repentance, especially if they are members of large churches. The pastor may have all the external marks of repentance but still suffer from serious character defects and concealed sin.

For this reason we must rely on the judgment of other leaders, men and women to whom the fallen leader is accountable. Is the pastor willing to cooperate with and submit to other leaders in the restoration process? And are those leaders willing to stand up to him/her? The fallen leader must be willing to be guided, directed, taught—to do anything that they think necessary to set his life in good order. If the fallen leader chooses to stand "alone before God," flee from him/her. He/she is dangerous. One purpose of a leader's restoration is the formation of mature character. A mature character is confirmed by a track record of resisting sin and walking faithfully with God, family and brothers and sisters.

ACCOUNTABILITY

Serious sins and character flaws require long track records of righteousness. For someone who has been unfaithful for years, the process requires long-term counseling and prayer. The key element for success is accountability; other leaders must be free to scrutinize the fallen leader's life and discern when true change has come, both for his/her benefit and for the benefit of those they may lead one day. The mechanics of restoration work a variety of ways. Most established denominations and churches have precise disciplinary procedures spelled out. The process may be overseen by leaders from the local body or leaders from outside the body, such as bishops. We need to be careful, though, relying too rigidly on disciplinary procedure. Each case is unique, requiring the love of God and Spirit-led wisdom for healing and restoration. The mechanics and oversight of the process are not as important as a willingness to submit on the part of the fallen leader and a willingness to confront and hold accountable on the part of those overseeing the process.

Many times after disciplining some leader in our flock, or in the Vineyard Movement, individuals will come to me and say, "Well, I'm going to remain accepting of this person because you guys are persecuting him." I've said, "We're not persecuting him. We're broken-hearted. But, the man (or woman) has sinned, and he/she isn't repentant. There's a major difference between being 'sorry that you did it' and 'sorry that you've been caught.'"

Sometimes under the banner of ministering mercy and grace to needy people, someone will say, "Well I'm not going to be judgmental!" Neither am I, but we have to keep a balance between truth and mercy. That's why the Scriptures encourages us to go tenderly when we have to deal with a brother or sister who's caught up in sin [Galatians 6:1].

We could take either position, feel justified in it and all the time subtly build walls between other brothers and sisters in Christ. As fallible human beings, we may understand more of one side than the other. I know because I used to preach against people like me. I thought, "Surely, those folks who speak in tongues can't be right because we're right! And we don't do that."

When the Lord gave me the gift of tongues (without me even asking for it), I had a real problem. Thank goodness God showed me my sin—accusations, prejudices, slander and bigotry. I'm still in process, and it's a slow process—ask my wife; she'll tell you—but I am making progress.

Christians cannot afford to sit by passively when their leaders fail. We have a responsibility to maintain an attitude of honor and respect toward them, avoiding gossip and bitterness that tears apart the Body of Christ and brings public scandal on the Gospel. But we also have a responsibility to call for fallen leaders' true repentance, accountability and a proven character before they are restored to leadership. How Christians treat their fallen leaders today will determine the vitality of the Church in the future.

Check out other books by John Wimber from Ampelon Publishing:

The Way in is the Way on by John Wimber.
The Way in is the Way On is a compilation of the late John Wimber's teachings and writings on life in Christ. In classic Wimber style, he captures the heart of the reader by sharing practical applications from the Bible that result in life-changing experiences with God.

To learn more, visit **ampelonpublishing.com**